The insights of an ancient Chinese general come to life.

"Sun Tzu's goal for writing *The Art of War* was not to glamorize warfare but to instruct military leaders in the best way to *end* an armed conflict as rapidly as possible or—even better—to prevent the outbreak of war in the first place.... These same ancient insights [give you] an effective, spiritual, and compassionate way to handle conflicts and intense competition in your life, and experience clarity of purpose and peace of mind, even in the most trying of circumstances."

—from the Introduction

Also Available in the SkyLight Illuminations Series

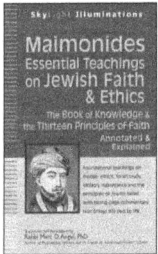

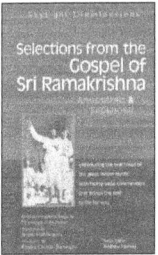

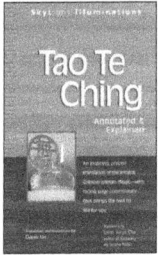

For more information about these and other SkyLight Paths books, please visit our website, www.skylightpaths.com.

Thomas Huynh is founder of www.sonshi.com, the Web's leading and most respected resource on Sun Tzu's *The Art of War*. He co-translated *The Art of War* with the Editors at Sonshi.com. He holds an MBA from Vanderbilt University.

Marc Benioff is chairman and CEO of Salesforce.com, the worldwide leader in on-demand business services. He has been a practitioner of Sun Tzu's principles for over a decade and is the coauthor of *The Business of Changing the World* and *Compassionate Capitalism*.

Thomas Cleary holds a PhD in East Asian Languages and Civilizations from Harvard University and a JD from the University of California, Berkeley. He is the translator of over seventy-five volumes of classical works from seven languages.

Sky Light Illuminations

Offers today's spiritual seeker an enjoyable entry into the great classic texts of the world's spiritual traditions. Each classic is presented in an accessible translation, with facing pages of guided commentary from experts, offering readers the keys they need to understand the history, context and meaning of the text. The series enables readers of all backgrounds to experience and understand classic spiritual texts directly, and to make them a part of their lives.

"Engaging commentaries and clear explanations.... Captures the essence of Sun Tzu's teachings and demonstrates how [this] ancient wisdom can be applied in the modern world to achieve powerful results."
—**Derek Lin,** author, *Tao Te Ching: Annotated & Explained*

"Insightful.... Check it out."
—*Businessweek* **Blog**

"Approachable and readable ... should take its place alongside the classic [translations].... A good addition to any library."
—**Defense and the National Interest Blog**

"Restore[s] Sun's place among spiritual classics of the East with this fresh, new annotated translation of a timely and perennially popular classic for a nonscholarly audience."
—*Library Journal*

Walking Together, Finding the Way®

SKYLIGHT PATHS®
PUBLISHING

www.skylightpaths.com

Find us on Facebook®
Facebook is a registered
trademark of Facebook, Inc.

The Art of War–
Spirituality
for Conflict

Other Books in the
SkyLight Illuminations Series

The Art of War–
Spirituality for Conflict

Annotated & Explained

Annotation by Thomas Huynh

Translation by Thomas Huynh and
the Editors of Sonshi.com

Foreword by Marc Benioff

Preface by Thomas Cleary

Walking Together, Finding the Way ®
SKYLIGHT PATHS®
PUBLISHING

The Art of War—Spirituality for Conflict:
Annotated & Explained

2016 Quality Paperback Edition, Fourth Printing

Annotation and introductory material © 2008 by Thomas Huynh
Foreword © 2008 by Marc Benioff
Preface © 2008 by Thomas Cleary

Library of Congress Cataloging-in-Publication Data
Huynh, Thomas.
The art of war—spirituality for conflict : annotated & explained / annotations by Thomas Huynh.
    p. cm.
Includes bibliographical references.
ISBN-13: 978-1-59473-244-7
ISBN-10: 1-59473-244-2
1. Peace–Religious aspects. 2. Conflict management–Religious aspects. 3. Sunzi, 6th cent. B.C. Sunzi bing fa. 4. Military art and science. 5. Strategy. I. Title.

BL65.P4H89 2008
355.02—dc22   2007052942
ISBN 978-1-59473-325-3 (eBook)

Manufactured in the United States of America

Cover design: Walter C. Bumford III
Cover art: © istockphoto.com/grahamnorris

SkyLight Paths Publishing is creating a place where people of different spiritual traditions come together for challenge and inspiration, a place where we can help each other understand the mystery that lies at the heart of our existence.

SkyLight Paths sees both believers and seekers as a community that increasingly transcends traditional boundaries of religion and denomination—people wanting to learn from each other, *walking together, finding the way.*

SkyLight Paths, "Walking Together, Finding the Way" and colophon are trademarks of LongHill Partners, Inc., registered in the U.S. Patent and Trademark Office.
Walking Together, Finding the Way®
Published by SkyLight Paths Publishing
www.skylightpaths.com

ISBN 978-1-68336-339-2 (hc.)

To my daughter, Victoria, and son, James—and all children—who will lead the world and set it right.

Contents ☐

Foreword □

by Marc Benioff

As the chairman and CEO of a technology company, I am always thinking about the future. It's somewhat ironic then, that the philosophies and
strategies I use to manage salesforce.com were written on slips of bamboo
2,500 years ago.

Larry Ellison, the CEO of Oracle Corporation and my mentor, first
introduced me to The Art of War, the Chinese military treatise by Sun Tzu,
when I was an executive at Oracle. Fundamentally, the book demonstrates how small armies can defeat larger ones. Larry applied its principles
to business with enthusiasm, and in growing Oracle from a small start-
up into one of the world's leading software companies, he proved the
enduring effectiveness of its insights even in modern circumstances. Sun
Tzu's treatise was originally written as a guide for generals in ancient
China, but I was amazed by its ability to transcend time and its relevance
to leaders of any mission.

So what does an age-old book about warfare and combat have to
do with business or personal interactions? A whole lot, it turns out. As
Thomas Huynh poignantly illustrates in *The Art of War—Spirituality for
Conflict: Annotated & Explained*, Sun Tzu may have been a general, but
he wasn't a warmonger. He was a leader defined by compassion and
spirituality, and he possessed a desire for resolution. The Art of War isn't
about war so much as it is about *the art of winning*.

Sun Tzu's original intention, as Huynh explains in the following pages,
was to teach a disadvantaged person or persons how to shift the balance
of power. Essentially, the book reveals how David can topple Goliath.
Since I first read The Art of War more than a dozen years ago, I have

applied its concepts to many areas of my life. The tenets of the book provided me with the confidence to enter an industry dominated by *much* bigger players—and gave us the strategies to render them powerless. Ultimately, it is how salesforce.com took on the entire software industry.

I started salesforce.com in 1999 with an idea to make purchasing and using notoriously onerous business software as simple as using a website like Yahoo! or Amazon.com. At first, we didn't have much more than a good idea. We launched the company in a one-bedroom rented apartment. Our servers were housed in a walk-in closet, our conference room was a balcony, and as we grew, the overflow went into my own apartment next door. (We hung Ethernet cable through the redwood trees to connect the two "offices".) We had no real office, no revenues, and no profits. We didn't even have a market—at that time, there were no phrases like "On-Demand" or "Software as a Service" to describe what we did.

We had very little compared to our competitors, but it didn't matter. (As Sun Tzu noted, having more resources does not ensure advantage.) What we lacked in terms of accepted ideas and impressive infrastructure, we made up for in energy and passion. We toiled away under pictures of the Dalai Lama and Albert Einstein. From my studies of Sun Tzu, I had learned both the importance of instilling inspiration and how to turn that vision into a reality: in Sun Tzu's own words, "One who knows how to unite upper and lower ranks in purpose will be victorious." I found the way to unite our "army" was to pursue an objective of great meaning that was accessible to the masses. We found that purpose with our "End of Software" mission. We were not just selling a Customer Relationship Management (CRM) tool, a service that would enable salespeople to sell more effectively—we were changing the way the software industry worked. We were committed to using the Internet to make software easier to use, less expensive, and more successful for our customers. We were evangelizing important values—democratizing an industry and embracing the way of the future.

Evoking innovation as inspiration was important, but there was another effort that was also a great unifier. To be truly successful, companies need to have a purpose bigger than making a profit. We created an integrated philanthropic model that gives 1 percent of our equity, 1 percent of our profits, and 1 percent of our employees' time to local and global nonprofit organizations. The Salesforce Foundation opened its first after-school technology center in San Francisco in July 2000 and has since created more than sixty technology centers and media programs in twelve countries where we have offices, including Japan, Ireland, and Singapore. The Foundation has also made meaningful contributions to disaster relief efforts in the United States and abroad. All of this was accomplished by the more than seventy thousand hours donated by our two thousand employees who embraced this effort with enthusiasm. By giving employees paid time off to volunteer, we have also seen a secondary gain. With an opportunity to do more than change the way businesses manage and share information, our employees have a greater sense of personal pride and satisfaction—and they are happier and therefore more productive at work.

While there have been modern critics of "compassionate capitalism," Sun Tzu understood that being practical and being compassionate are not mutually exclusive. In fact, it is self-serving to be compassionate, he said, for preserving a defeated army intact helps quell resentment—and ease later interactions. We've found this wisdom to be true. How can we thrive as a company if the community we operate in falters? We can't: many of our employees, partners, customers, and shareholders come from the communities the Foundation serves. We need to ensure that our local community succeeds for us to succeed and we need to ensure that our global community thrives for us to grow. Acting in a way that is both practical and compassionate has proved to be a secret weapon for success.

Another pivotal strategy for success was to remain aware of our surroundings and adaptable to change. Instead of fighting change, like many of our opponents, we greeted it. This was our mantra from the beginning when countless people told us an On-Demand premise would never work. A key figure in the CRM industry even proclaimed, audaciously, that our young company would fail within a year. Nevertheless, we decided to pursue the idea, and ultimately came to compete against this dominant player.

Sun Tzu advised a cool and rational approach to conflict, but this particular adversary took the battle for business personally, which put him and his company at a disadvantage. Since our start-up was too small to overpower the competition, we had to devise creative ways to outsmart them; many of the strategies stoked our adversary's emotions. One time, we placed people outside their annual conference to peacefully wave signs that said "NO SOFTWARE" and "The Internet Is Really Neat … Software Is Obsolete!" Rather than coolly seeing this as a business and marketing tactic, their executives reacted emotionally and called the police—only adding fuel to the fire and garnering more press for us. Another time we rented all the taxis our competitors needed to get to a conference in Europe. Even their executives were left with no choice other than to take our rides, which we provided as a free service, but we also decorated the vehicles with "NO SOFTWARE" logos and filled them with our literature. They were caught by complete surprise. We realized that Sun Tzu's strategy to "appear at places where he must rush to defend, and rush to places where he least expects" works in different kinds of battles in different kinds of times. While for several years we remained just a flea to the elephant of our competitor, we sure made the elephant dance. It was all homage to The Art of War: "Those skilled in warfare move the enemy, and are not moved by the enemy."

While much of our business strategy has been defined by the principles of The Art of War, my personal interactions have as well. In fact, salesforce.com may never have been created, or at least would look very different, had I not followed its wisdom. Shortly after I decided to launch salesforce.com, I found three talented engineers to build the technology. They had a successful business—Left Coast Software—stable salaries, and the security to fastidiously select their next move, but they agreed to talk with me about my idea. When I first met to interview one of them, Dave Moellenhoff, he began to openly disparage some of my past products! I was surprised by what he was saying, but I recalled Sun Tzu's words "He who is quick tempered can be insulted," and refused to get bent out of shape. Instead, I politely disagreed with his assessment. Later, Dave told me that his attack was just a test to see how I would convince people of our idea and respond to criticism. Whereas I had thought I was interviewing him, he had turned the tables to test me. By following Sun Tzu's strategies and remaining non-emotional, I proved my capabilities and avoided catastrophe. Following Sun Tzu's principles in this way is ultimately how I found the right business partners, built a company with a compassionate culture, and eventually achieved victory in the marketplace.

You do not have to be in the military, or politics, or business, to benefit from the counsel in this text. Its insights can be applied in any situation that needs resolution and works even in interpersonal quests. As Sun Tzu observed, "One who knows the enemy and knows himself will not be in danger in a hundred battles." Every mantra—from keeping your cool, to being patient, to finding your opening—represents a tactic that when wisely applied can dictate a winning strategy.

As a devotee of The Art of War I wish that I had had Thomas Huynh's edition, *The Art of War—Spirituality for Conflict: Annotated & Explained*, when I was first studying Sun Tzu. Huynh has dedicated the past twenty years to studying this text and founded Sonshi.com, the Web's leading resource on The Art of War (another testament to the text transcending time!). He and the editors of Sonshi.com have painstakingly translated and impeccably researched this version. With insight on how the strategies were used in ancient China, as well as referencing concepts from Buddhism, Taoism, Judaism, and Christianity, this book demonstrates how Sun Tzu's wisdom bridges many seemingly diverse ideas and ultimately connects us by illuminating our shared values.

What's most unique is that this edition is translated and explained through the lens of true compassion. Huynh, who came to the United

States as a political refugee when he was seven years old, knows the horrors of war first hand. A noted scholar and wise reconciler, Huynh believes Sun Tzu's text is the greatest book in the world because it has the answer to promoting wisdom, spirituality, hope—and ending the need for war, which Huynh views as "the most cruel, destructive, and mindless human activity." A countless number of us wish for peace, and there is room and reason for more to join this crusade. The insight we can learn from this text, and the contributions we can make guided by it, can enrich each and all of our lives.

Preface ☐

by Thomas Cleary

There are three times when the world is deranged:
during the course of an epidemic,
in the chaos of war,
and on the voiding of verbal contracts.

Senchus Mor

According to a Buddhist maxim, "All things have their function—it's a matter of use in the appropriate situation." The importance of understanding what is appropriate according to circumstances is graphically illustrated in a Taoist story on the arts of peace and war:

A certain man had two sons, one of whom was fond of study, the other fond of arms. The studious one offered his arts to the lord of a certain state, who hired him to tutor his princes. The military scientist went to another state and offered his science to the lord of that domain. The lord was pleased with him, and made him a military director. The salaries of the two sons enriched their family, and their ranks brought glory to their parents.

Now, the neighbor also had two sons who pursued the same professions, but they were impoverished. Envying what their successful neighbors had, they inquired how to get ahead. The first man's sons told them the facts.

The neighbor's scholarly son then went to a certain state to put his arts at the service of the lord. The lord said, "At present the lords are fighting each other, so their only concerns are armaments and food. If I tried to govern my state with benevolent ideals, this would be a way to destruction." So the lord had him castrated and banished.

The neighbor's military-minded son went to another state, where he sought to put his science at the service of the lord. The lord said, "Mine is a weak state, and it is hemmed in between large states. I render service to larger states, while aiding smaller states—this is the way to security. If I rely on military strategy, I can expect to be annihilated. And now if I send you back in one piece, you might go to another state and cause me some serious trouble." So he had his feet hacked off and sent him back home.

When they got back, the two sons went next door with their father, beating their breasts and complaining. The man whose sons had succeeded said, "Those whose timing is right flourish, while those whose timing is off perish. Your pursuits are the same as ours, but your results were different from ours. This was because your timing was off, not because your practices were mistaken.

"No principle in the world is always right, and no thing is always wrong. What was used yesterday may be rejected today, what is rejected now may be used later on. This use or disuse has no fixed right or wrong. To avail yourself of opportunities at just the right time, responding to events without being set in your ways, is in the domain of wisdom. If your wisdom is insufficient, even if you are widely learned and highly skilled, you'll come to an impasse wherever you go."

Perhaps unexpectedly, the "appropriate situation" to which Sun Tzu's ancient The Art of War applies includes our own age, and extends beyond the military to the civil realm. To be sure, the idea that competition and conflict are natural, normative, even inevitable in human endeavors has gained widespread consensus in many domains of theory and practice. Yet the usefulness of The Art of War in civil concerns does not require the preeminence of a paradigm of conflict, however suitable this may seem to Sun Tzu's ostensible theme. The Art of War derives its persuasiveness in contexts other than armed conflict through its focus on practical matters such as leadership, organization, the gathering and use of information, contingency planning, efficient decision making, and awareness—all matters essential to any constructive or collaborative undertaking, military or otherwise. This broad application of Sun Tzu's strategic principles to a variety of circumstances is precisely what Thomas Huynh explores in *The Art of War—Spirituality for Conflict: Annotated & Explained.*

Planning, Efficiency, Awareness

The Art of War is particularly suited to this cross-disciplinary, contemporary application because the extensive use of analogy, typical of the traditions of Chinese language, literature, and philosophy from which Sun-Tzu's The Art of War emerged, facilitates the export of ideas and principles from one domain of endeavor to others. In the case of this particular classic, it may be said that the book's *context of crisis*—of which war serves as a general symbol as well as a specific embodiment—highlights especially the benefits of optimizing contingency planning and decision-making efficiency proportionately to the narrowing of tolerable margins of error, in any number of particular contexts.

More specifically, one of the most fundamental principles of contingency planning to be found in both military and civil classics, even in manuals of psychological and spiritual advice, is not to forget danger in times of ease, not to forget emergency in times of normalcy. In other words: Be prepared. In more leisurely times, formulating a strategic system such as the one offered in The Art of War as an adaptable frame of reference can assist in organizing and accelerating planning and decision-making processes when contexts of crisis do arise.

It is the unique genius of a typical technique of analogy used in traditional Chinese philosophies, which may be described structurally as a progression of scale, that allows for such flexibility. The essential design of this conceptual device consists of expanding and embedding spheres of context, an exercise that can be used to study and understand the connections, causes, and consequences of events—a necessary procedure in planning, whatever the context. A prime example of this is the simple analogy of the role of the mind in the body to that of the ruler in the nation—as the mind guides the body, so the ruler guides the country—a construct customarily applied in a wide range of contexts from politics and economics to moral philosophy and medical theory.

The discourse on warfare in the Taoist classic *Master of the Hidden Storehouse* illustrates this art of connecting literal and figurative expression to achieve specific cognitive effects by systematically expanding attention and awareness: "When you look into the signs of war, you find they are in the mind. When there is unexpressed anger in the heart, this is already war! Hateful looks and angry faces are war; boastful words and shoving matches are war. Exaggerated contention and aggressive combat are war." As these words suggest, observing and considering the conditions of, and changes in, the psychological interface within and between varying levels of conflict, from the subtle to the gross, can lay the foundation for sensible and strategic approaches to achieve resolution.

Three Models of Unity in Overcoming Conflict

The contrast between concord and discord, from petty grievances between individuals to grave conflicts between nations, is conventionally represented in terms of agreement or disagreement, or the unity or difference of views. This question of unity between parties, or the lack of it, lies at the heart of conflict and is the key to resolving it. Where unity is missing between individuals, the resolution may be simple, but where diversity of interest is dictated by the underlying social, economic, political, or other structure of an interaction or relation, the problem of consensus and cooperation can become correspondingly complex.

In the historical context of The Art of War, a time of intense competition and conflict, there were already competing conceptions of the very idea of unity itself, conceived in response to the political, cultural, and intellectual diversity of the age.

One influential concept for achieving unity proposed the eradication of diversity, as suggested in a discourse on "nonduality" in the *Annals of Mr. Lu*, attributed to one of the strategic forefathers of Chinese imperialism. In it, the author suggests that even the diverse teachings of the sages were inherently contradictory and therefore dangerous:

> If you govern a country by listening to the arguments of a multitude of people, the country will be in danger in no time at all. How do we know this is so? Lao-tzu emphasized flexibility, Confucius emphasized humaneness, Mo-tzu emphasized universality, the Keeper of the Pass emphasized purity, Lieh-tzu emphasized emptiness, Ch'en Ping emphasized equality, Yang Chu emphasized self, Sun Pin emphasized power, Wang Liao emphasized initiative, Ni Liang emphasized conformism.
>
> Using bells and drums is a means of unifying ears; making law and order uniform is a way of unifying minds. When the smart ones can't be clever and the stupid ones can't be clumsy, this is a means of unifying a mass. When the brave ones can't go ahead and the fearful ones can't follow behind, this is a means of unifying efforts.
>
> So with unity there is order; with difference there is disorder. With unity there is safety, with difference there is danger. Who but a sage can equalize myriad dissimilarities, so that the stupid and the smart, the skillful and the clumsy, all work fully to the best of their ability, as if coming from a single opening.

The first emperor of China, executing his interpretation of this idea of unity, felt it necessary to have books burned and scholars buried to enforce uniformity. If not for its short-term effectiveness, the extremes of violence and repression employed to impose a totalitarian regime such as this might be sufficient indication of its unnatural character and inevitable failure.

But predicting, perceiving, and trying to prevent the problems associated with enforcing an absolutist form of unity may result in an exaggerated individualism that leads to equally troubling problems, such as ignorant intolerance, irrational antagonism rooted in subjective complacency, and intellectual isolation. These may likewise be found illustrated in Taoist teachings, as related with characteristic demulcent humor in the classic of Lieh-tzu, where each personification of negative human traits wallows in self-imposed and self-congratulatory seclusion:

Ink Spiller, Fanatic, Lazy, and Hasty traveled the world together, each doing as he liked. To the end of their years they never knew each others' state of mind, as each one thought his own wisdom most profound.

Tricky, Simple, Artless, and Fawning traveled the world together, each doing as he liked. To the end of their years they never spoke to each other, as each one thought his own skill most subtle.

Withdrawn, Candid, Stammerer, and Scold traveled the world together, each doing as he liked. To the end of their years they never understood each other, as each one thought his own talent adequate.

Con-Man, Buck-Passer, Bold, and Timid traveled the world together, each doing as he liked. To the end of their years they never criticized each other, because each one thought his own conduct unobjectionable.

Conformist, Individualist, Opportunist, and Independent traveled the world together, each doing as he liked. To the end of their years they never paid attention to each other, each one thinking himself in harmony with the times.

There are a multiplicity of attitudes. They are not the same in appearance, but all are alike in that they wind up saying it was their destiny.

Such deterioration of diversity into fragmentation through unexamined subjectivity and lapse in communication foments division, friction, and conflict, and results in impoverishment of thought and perspective, as well as analogous restriction of other resources.

Fortunately there is another perspective on achieving unity, which already existed in the age of The Art of War and has been revived from time to time when the momentum of the absolutist approach exhausted itself. It is a dynamic unity that both recognizes the validity of individual perspectives and seeks to align those views toward a common, larger goal. This is vividly exemplified in a lesson from another famous book of the Warring States Era known as *Shih-tzu*. Here, through an expanded horizon that leads to impartiality, individual perspectives are capable of critical reflection, and even apparently contradictory doctrines can be appreciated for complementary contributions under a single, greater purpose and truth:

> If you looked at the stars from inside a well, no more than a few stars would be visible to you. If you look from a hilltop, then you can see when they first appear and when they fade away. It's not that they're any brighter, but the setting makes it this way.
>
> Now then, subjectivity is the inside of the well, impartiality is the top of the hill. Thus when intelligence rides on subjectivity, it knows little; when it rides on impartiality, it knows a lot.
>
> How do we know this is so? The countries of Wu and Yueh immolate servants and concubines on the death of their masters; when people of the central states hear of this, they think it's wrong. And yet when they themselves are enraged, they'll sacrifice kith and kin for a single word. When their intelligence is impartial, then they care about the servants and concubines of Wu and Yueh, but when subjective they forget their own kith and kin. It's not that their intelligence diminishes, but that anger covers it.
>
> Liking also does that. As the proverb goes, no one recognizes faults in his own son. It's not that intelligence is diminished, but it is covered up by affection.
>
> For this reason, whoever would discourse on relative values and define right and wrong must speak thereof from an impartial mind, and listen thereunto with an impartial mind. Only then is it possible to know.
>
> Ordinary people love their families rather than their neighbors; lords love their states rather than their rivals; a son of heaven includes the whole world in the magnitude of his love.
>
> Mo-tzu emphasized universality, Confucius emphasized public interest, Huang-tzu emphasized truthfulness, T'ien-tzu emphasized equality, Lieh-tzu emphasized openness, Liao-tzu emphasized distinguishing interests. These schools have been contradicting each other for generations now, all of them covered by subjectivity.... If we had universality, public interest, emptiness, equality, truthfulness, simplicity, and distinguishing interests all as one truth, then they would not contradict one another.

Thomas Huynh's *The Art of War—Spirituality for Conflict: Annotated & Explained* argues for just such an impartial middle way, a path described by Sun Tzu that can still orient varied perspectives under the common, humane goal of ending all manner of conflict as rapidly, and compassionately, as possible.

> *Is this one of ours, or a stranger—so calculate the small-minded;*
> *To those of noble conduct, the whole world is the family.*

Hitopadesa

Introduction ☐

Two decades ago, in a small bookstore in Seattle, Washington, a little black book caught my attention. Its title was simple: *The Art of War.*[1] The book had been written in 512 BCE by a relatively obscure Chinese scholar and military general named Sun Tzu,[2] and that particular edition had been translated by Thomas Cleary. Although I wasn't particularly interested in military studies, I had heard of Sun Tzu a few years before, and the title made me curious to learn more. I picked up the book and began leafing through it.

Before long, my curiosity turned to fascination and I sat down on the hard floor, absorbed in page after page of compelling observations that, despite the book's title, seemed to be more about wisdom than about combat:

> Those who win every battle are not really skillful—those who render others' armies helpless without fighting are the best of all.

> So the rule is not to count on opponents not coming but to rely on having ways of dealing with them.

> Anger can revert to joy, wrath can revert to delight, but a nation destroyed cannot be restored to existence, and the dead cannot be restored to life.[3]

By the time I had finished browsing the book, I realized what I had in my hands was something truly special. As a military treatise, The Art of War has withstood the test of time. (It is still required reading in military academies across the world.) And its strategies prove effective in other settings as well—a trip to the management or finance section of any bookstore will quickly reveal a plethora of titles applying Sun Tzu's teachings to the highly competitive world of business. But for me, the book's appeal went deeper. I wasn't in the military or in business, yet Sun Tzu's words resonated with my own life. Here, compressed into thirteen short chapters, was profound insight of a spiritual nature that could help me live my everyday life unconstrained by conflict, either with others or within myself.

These same ancient insights are available to everyone, whatever spiritual path you are on, or none at all. *The Art of War—Spirituality for Conflict: Annotated & Explained* is for you if you want to learn an effective, spiritual, and compassionate way to handle conflicts and intense competition in your life, and to experience clarity of purpose and peace of mind, even in the most trying of circumstances.

Spirituality from a War Manual?

In 1999, after an intense decade of studying The Art of War, I founded Sonshi.com (*Sonshi* is the English transliteration of the Japanese form of the name *Sun Tzu*), which has become the Internet's leading resource on Sun Tzu's The Art of War[4] and is the only site to have the endorsement of every major The Art of War translator and commentator alive today— over forty in all.

My goal for Sonshi.com was to help correct the widespread belief that The Art of War is a treatise only on how to successfully conduct a military campaign. It is that, of course—Sun Tzu was a general, after all— but this is only part of the picture. Sun Tzu was no warmonger, or "hawk" as we might say today. Rather, Sun Tzu viewed war *at best* as a destructive and grievous last resort when all other options fail—at worst, as an utter failure of strategy and leadership, and a dereliction of duty. Sun Tzu never saw war as a cause for celebration, or even satisfaction, because of the terrible price exacted from everyone involved.

Sun Tzu's goal in writing The Art of War was not to glamorize warfare but to instruct military leaders in the best way to *end* an armed conflict as rapidly as possible or—even better—to prevent the outbreak of war in the first place. When Sun Tzu spoke of victory, this is what he meant—the prevention or quick resolution of conflict, not the conquering of your opponent.

Sun Tzu's purpose may surprise you, given the title of the book. My older brother, who has received advanced degrees in religious studies, used to wonder why I study The Art of War—shouldn't I study The Art of Peace instead? And yet in a very real sense, achieving the art of peace was precisely Sun Tzu's goal for writing The Art of War, because understanding the nature of conflict can help you stop it. An analogous example might be drawn from the field of medicine. If you want to find a cure for cancer, you must know everything about cancer: what it is, why it exists, who it affects, how it behaves, where it spreads. With this knowledge, you have a tremendous advantage in stopping cancer. Without this knowledge, you are helpless. Similarly, you can only end conflict if you diligently study and understand it.

For Sun Tzu, the fundamental mechanism to ending conflict is to achieve a massive imbalance of power and resources over your opponent, and then to leverage that imbalance so skillfully and decisively that your foe is utterly overwhelmed and chooses to surrender rather than fight.

When such a scenario succeeds, life and property are preserved and genuine harmony can be reestablished by winning your adversary's respect and loyalty through acts of sincere kindness. It is not easy, but in the long run it ensures a lasting peace. This approach may sound questionable, or even naive, until you consider the alternative: merely conquering your opponent through violence and brute force may be easier and successful in the short run, but such an approach only plants the seeds of resentment and further conflict. This lesson is as true today in our modern world as it was in Sun Tzu's time and before.

Merely having more resources at your disposal doesn't necessarily translate into an advantage over your opponent, for such things can be easily squandered through negligence, arrogance, or foolhardiness. To accomplish a truly peaceful resolution, you need skill, creativity, and a sense of selflessness. These traits help you succeed even when you are at a material disadvantage. The Art of War shows you how to leverage the strength you do have to shift the balance of power in your favor. Sun Tzu's original intended audience were those on the weaker side of a struggle for power—he wanted to teach a person or group in the position of disadvantage how to turn the tables so that they could occupy the advantageous position.

The Enduring Relevance for Each of Us

Conflict arises in each of our lives. You don't have to be in high-pressure occupations such as the military or business to appreciate the drain on energy, resources, and morale that extended conflict can claim. The good news is that Sun Tzu's principles work equally well in any situation of conflict, whatever the circumstances and whoever the players.

Sun Tzu's overarching goal for The Art of War was to describe the best way to prevent (not avoid) conflicts in the first place and the best way to prevail as quickly as possible with minimal loss of life and property if a conflict did arise. Many of the specific methods he describes to achieve this goal are, at their core, surprisingly spiritual in nature. In fact, many of his insights find parallel teachings—albeit in different contexts—in some of the world's great religious traditions such as Taoism, Christianity, Judaism, and Buddhism. I refer to some of these principles throughout the book, so it is worthwhile to briefly describe some of the most important ones here.

Perhaps the most foundational of these insights is the importance of maintaining an objective emotional *detachment* when calculating your position relative to your adversary's. Being ruled by your emotions, exaggerating your strengths, denying your weaknesses, and wishful thinking can only lead to catastrophe. But maintaining your impartiality will allow you to see your circumstances with clarity and will provide opportunities to make sound decisions and respond to changing circumstances appropriately.

In this way, Sun Tzu's vision of detachment bears a striking resemblance to the Buddhist concept of the same name, which encourages you to step back and observe your emotions nonjudgmentally (neither exaggerating nor denying them) while letting them pass of their own accord, all with the ultimate purpose of seeing reality as it is, not as you wish it to be.

Sun Tzu also advocated *flexibility* because it represents true strength in a changing environment. Taoists have long honored the value of flexibility, teaching that rigidity may be a strength in some situations, but can be a liability when circumstances change. A rigid building may be solid, but under the stress of an earthquake its lack of pliancy may cause it to crumble, whereas a tree standing next to it can bend and flex to absorb the shock and therefore remain intact. Flexibility in our lives means having a fundamental ability to relate to any new environment and excel in it. Instead of fighting it, you greet it with open arms and observe it; instead of criticizing it, you caress it and understand it; instead of ignoring it, you make it yours and be one with it. This Taoist principle is as helpful today as it has always been.

Another spiritual principle underlying Sun Tzu's work has to do with your attitude toward your opponent, who in this context is someone who not only hinders your progress toward a goal but also does so with malicious intent. Throughout The Art of War, Sun Tzu highlights two specific attributes that often plague your adversaries: anger and greed. These motives are self-serving and (should) contrast with your own motivation. This distinction is important because anyone can read The Art of War, but only the benevolent can truly extract Sun Tzu's principles fully. Behind his seemingly cold, explicit strategies, Sun Tzu's implicit *spiritual and universal love*—even for his enemies—warms the book's pages. Along the lines of Jesus's proclamation, "Love your enemies, do good to those who hate you" (Luke 6:27), Sun Tzu's aim wasn't to destroy but to preserve. Sun Tzu treated his soldiers like his own children, caring for their health and well-being. Captured enemy spies and soldiers weren't killed, but rather were treated well and incorporated into his own army. His generous benevolence ultimately protected his people more effectively than ruthlessness, because it sealed the people's loyalty and commitment, secured the respect of the enemy, and augmented the army, thereby even further increasing his advantage in strength over the opposition.

Sun Tzu's *compassion* even extended to the point of allowing a defeated army to return home instead of crushing it. But he was simultaneously *pragmatic*. Throughout The Art of War, the strategies he proposes seem to answer two questions: First, is this practical? Second, is this compassionate? To Sun Tzu, the two are not mutually exclusive. From a narrowly pragmatic point of view, utterly destroying an enemy would, at least temporarily, remove any worries about negotiation, compromise, or reconciliation, and might seem to be the more effective solution. This approach clearly fails the test of the second question, "Is this compassionate?"; but, ultimately, it also fails the test of the first question, for no conquest motivated by hatred or revenge is ever complete. In time the enemy, fueled by the very ruthlessness of the conqueror's former actions, will gain strength and renew the struggle. So only a solution that is simultaneously compassionate and pragmatic can instill a lasting peace.

Another core element underlying Sun Tzu's work is the necessity for a keen sense of *foresight*. Sun Tzu asserts that "those who are skilled in warfare gained victory where victory was easily gained"—that is, those who possess genuine wisdom know how to solve problems while they are still small and simple—before they develop into larger, more difficult problems. Solving large, difficult problems may earn you a reputation for skillful negotiation, but Sun Tzu asserts that this supposed achievement is actually a form of failure, and having true wisdom means preventing difficult problems from arising in the first place. Ironically, this highest form of efficacy will often go unnoticed by many people, since the leader's work seems so effortless and subtle. This foresight may not earn you a great reputation, but Sun Tzu also believed that bravery and greatness involve shunning what other people think of you, both praise and criticism, and doing what you believe is the right thing. A brave person forgoes his or her own ego and well-being, and acts with neither fear of punishment nor expectation of reward. Some people call these traits *humility* and *courage*. To Sun Tzu they are merely labels that describe an effective and honorable way of living everyday life.

Finally, Sun Tzu was *deliberate* in his actions. He didn't depend on omens or the supernatural to tell him what to do—he deemed that those are for people who don't want to think for themselves. Instead, he depended on himself to calculate a sound strategy from relevant information obtained firsthand from the source. According to Sun Tzu, extraordinary achievements can be realized through reliable, ordinary means.

Sun Tzu's wisdom shows us that although conflict is inevitable, we can end all conflict quickly and compassionately through wisdom and benevolence. When two sides who consider each other enemies converge in armed struggle, for the moment they are no longer enemies. They are fellow human beings who face the same two choices that their ancestors did for centuries before them: *to destroy each other or to prosper together*. Sun Tzu began his The Art of War urging that we examine our conflicts carefully. If we truly follow his advice, the better choice becomes clear. It is never too late to fulfill our duty to make the right decision for ourselves and for those around us.

The World's Best-Kept Secret?

Military secrets are usually closely guarded. So you might question why I would promote a book on strategy that gives advantage to any reader who applies its principles. Don't I want to keep the book a secret so that all my own personal adversaries won't be able to subvert me?

It is true that the Japanese samurai and Chinese generals frequently gained insight from the text before every battle, and so for many centuries The Art of War was kept from public access. I, however, have a different view, one that I think is perfectly in line with Sun Tzu's teachings: I want to share his principles with as many people as possible, *especially* my adversaries.

If I alone understand Sun Tzu's strategies, I may indeed prevail in a fight over my opponent. But if we *both* understand Sun Tzu's teachings, chances are much better that one side will realize, after determining the factors necessary for success, that fighting is futile because it is outmatched. In this way, a fight is more easily prevented altogether and the resources of both sides are preserved.

This logic did not escape Chinese president Hu Jintao, who on April 20, 2006, personally gave President George W. Bush and other U.S. officials copies of Sun Tzu's The Art of War. For the sake of both countries, I sincerely hope they read it.

Historical Context

Who was this man behind The Art of War? Sun Tzu (544–496 BCE)[5] was a Chinese military general and philosopher who lived during a tumultuous time in China near the end of the Spring and Autumn period (770–476 BCE). Sun was his family name and Tzu was his honorary title. Thus, the literal meaning of *Sun Tzu* is "Master Sun." His birth name was Wu.

During the Spring and Autumn period, China consisted of over 150 factional states that vied for supremacy under a weak Chou dynasty. They engaged in intense and constant battle until only thirteen major states remained. Of the thirteen states, seven possessed vastly superior troops and resources over the other six, setting the stage for further warfare and consolidation in the Warring States period (475–221 BCE).

Sun Tzu was born into a noble family from the state of Ch'i; his grandfather was a provincial governor, his father an accomplished military general. Through his father, he had firsthand knowledge of the inner workings of the Chinese army, whose troops usually numbered in the hundreds of thousands by the end of the Spring and Autumn period. This knowledge, coupled with his engaged study and readings of past battles, helped him to gain a reputation as a brilliant strategist at an early age.

Due to the recommendation of a trusted imperial advisor who mentioned Sun Tzu's name no fewer than seven times, the king of the Wu state, Ho Lu, finally relented and met with Sun Tzu. It was at this meeting that Sun Tzu presented his book The Art of War. He was only thirty years old. Impressed by the book, Ho Lu subsequently hired Sun Tzu to formulate strategies that later aided the relatively small Wu state to capture Ying, the capital city of the vastly superior state of Ch'u, and to hold back imminent advances from Ch'i, Chin, and Yueh. Because of Sun Tzu's stunning successes, his name quickly spread throughout China such that his reputation remains intact today, 2,500 years later.

What happened to Sun Tzu after his employment with Ho Lu, or how he died, is unknown. The only subsequent entry in China's historical records was found in the *Yueh Chueh Shu* ("The End of the Kingdom of Yueh") declaring, "Outside of the city gate of Wu is a large tomb—the tomb of the King of Wu's foreign official, Sun Tzu—which lies ten miles from the country. He was [an] expert at military strategy."[6]

The original manuscript of The Art of War given to Ho Lu no longer exists, so we cannot ascertain whether changes were later made to the main text by scribes. However, a comparison of the earliest known copy of The Art of War (ca. 140 BCE) with the official Sung dynasty copy produced one thousand years later shows no significant differences.

The scribes did add "Sun Tzu said," to the beginning of every chapter, implying that The Art of War was a collection of verbal instructions. But this is not entirely accurate. Ssu-ma Ch'ien (145–ca. 86 BCE), "the father of Chinese history,"[7] recorded that Ho Lu said to Sun Tzu, "I have read your thirteen chapters, Sir, in their entirety."[8] Ho Lu's statement confirms that Sun Tzu's original book was, in fact, a written work composed of thirteen chapters, just like the editions we have today. The mention of Sun Tzu's "sayings" connotes the heavy emphasis the ancient Chinese placed on learning lessons from speech, since very few people were literate. Even Sun Tzu had to later clarify his book to Ho Lu with an oral presentation.

Sun Tzu was an academician first and a warrior second. This order of skill progression may seem odd to the Western world, but twentieth-century Asian leaders such Mao Tse Tung and Ho Chi Minh—both avid students of Sun Tzu's The Art of War—followed a similar path. Mao Tse Tung based his *On Guerrilla Warfare* on The Art of War, at times copying the verses almost verbatim; Ho Chi Minh translated The Art of War for his Vietnamese officers.[9] Their backgrounds resembled those of college professors more than military generals. Despite their lack of first-hand experience in wars, Mao Tse Tung and Ho Chi Minh devised strategies in the Chinese Civil War (1927–1949) and the battle of Dien Bien Phu (1953–1954), respectively, two classic military case studies illustrating the strategic brilliance that enables a weaker side to defy the odds and win against a much stronger side.

As mentioned, Sun Tzu's reputation for wisdom in warfare was immense, and so it was not surprising that his book was soon treasured by those who wished to learn from him. It has remained in continual use since its appearance 2,500 years ago; unlike the fate of many Chinese works, The Art of War has never been lost or destroyed. Famous Chinese military strategists such as Cao Cao and Zhuge Liang of the Three Kingdoms period (184–280 CE) employed and commented on the book's verses. During the Sung dynasty (960–1279 CE), it was made part of The Seven Military Classics, prerequisite reading for the imperial examinations that were required in order to become a ranking government official. The Japanese, through frequent knowledge-building trips to China, incorporated the book into their repertoire as early as 400 CE. Two of the best-known strategists of feudal Japan, Minamoto Yoshitsune (1159–1189 CE) and Takeda Shingen (1521–1573 CE), made The Art of War their main text of choice.

It would be over two millennia until The Art of War made its way from China into Western civilization. Father J. J. M. Amiot, a French Jesuit priest who lived in China, translated the work into French in 1772. This gave many scholars valid reason to speculate that Napoleon Bonaparte, France's preeminent military general and emperor, read and employed Sun Tzu's strategies in his battles. In fact, Napoleon was a voracious reader of military works and Amiot's translation was an instant bestseller, so for Napoleon to have somehow excluded The Art of War from his long reading list would seem improbable.

The first English translation of The Art of War came from British officer Captain E. F. Calthrop, who rendered it while studying in Japan in 1905. (Accordingly, he titled the work *Sonshi*.) Today, Sun Tzu's The Art of War has been translated into every major language in the world, and the number of editions grows every year.

Some notable individuals who were demonstrably influenced by The Art of War are Colin Powell, George Patton, Vo Nguyen Giap, Che Guevara, Akira Kurosawa, Bruce Lee, Ronald Reagan, John Murtha, Mike Huckabee, Robert Gates, Marc Benioff, Larry Ellison, Bill Belichick, Dusty Baker, George Steinbrenner, Pat Riley, and Tupac Shakur. This list of famous names from fields as diverse as the military, professional sports, and the music industry, reflects how Sun Tzu's book can be applied in various endeavors with equal relevancy. The typical student of The Art of War, however, is rarely known outside of his or her domain. This student is an ordinary individual who simply wants to effect a positive change within his or her household, company, neighborhood, or community.

How This Book Is Organized

With so many The Art of War editions available nowadays, what makes *The Art of War—Spirituality for Conflict* any different and better? This book is the product of twenty years of dedicated scholarship and application of The Art of War, of working with over forty of the most reputable authors and scholars of The Art of War over the years, and of fielding thousands of questions from readers at Sonshi.com since its founding. Although I explain every important verse individually, all explanations are given in the context of Sun Tzu's main driving purpose. I also do not shrink away from discussing some of Sun Tzu's more controversial ideas, such as deception and spies, and why they—like all of Sun Tzu's concepts—are critical components of the strategy to overcome your adversaries and possibly make them your allies. I'll explore how even these seemingly unsavory aspects of Sun Tzu's philosophy can be compatible with a spiritual approach to conflict. (Hint: the key lies in your motivation.)

This book is divided into thirteen chapters, which reflects Sun Tzu's original division of The Art of War. Each chapter focuses on a primary theme or element of strategy, just like Sun Tzu's original work. However, it's important to note that reading The Art of War isn't a simple step-by-step approach to conflict management. Rather, Sun Tzu synthesized his insights in an organic way, sometimes building on previous concepts, sometimes repeating information, sometimes relying on the reader to interpret and reflect on his poetic, shorthand manner of describing things. In this way, The Art of War itself is somewhat deceptive: it is short enough to be read in an afternoon, but subtle and nuanced enough to be studied for years, decades, a lifetime.

In chapter 1, "Calculations," Sun Tzu presents five chief factors that determine the outcome in any conflict. By knowing these factors, you can predict whether you'll be able to overcome your adversary even before you take the first step. Chapter 2, "Doing Battle," discusses the heavy toll you would incur should you want to confront your adversary. If you must, the chapter advises you to act swiftly, to avoid running out of energy and resources. In chapter 3, "Planning Attacks," you will learn that the highest excellence is winning without fighting, not decimating every adversary you encounter. Since destruction clearly isn't your goal and victory is, leaving things intact maximizes your gains and helps you to mend your fences with your adversary. In chapter 4, "Formation," you will learn the importance of early preparation and securing a position of invincibility.

Chapter 5, "Force," explains the concept of achieving unstoppable momentum through concentration and variability (mixing common and uncommon methods). Chapter 6, "Weakness and Strength," shows you how to overcome your adversary even if you are the weaker side. Through formlessness—being imperceptible to the opposite side—you can surmount even the most powerful of adversaries. Chapter 7, "Armed Struggle," describes how to manage your hardship when you must actively go forth to confront your adversary. Despite this difficulty, Sun Tzu shows you how to conserve your energy. Chapter 8, "Nine Changes," describes how you will be able to keep your strategy ever relevant to the problem at hand through adapting and being flexible to contingencies. In chapter 9, "Army Maneuvers," Sun Tzu advocates the need to carefully observe your environment and the subtle actions of your adversary so you can avoid disaster and secure an advantage.

Chapters 10 and 11, "Ground Formation" and "Nine Grounds," respectively, define and outline strategies for sixteen types of grounds, which represent the environment you and your adversary operate in, including the freedoms and limitations in each environment. In chapter 12, "Fire Attacks," Sun Tzu explains special attacks that disrupt and provoke—their inherent dangers as well as their benefits. Finally, chapter 13, "Using Spies," explores the five types of spies and discusses how invaluable they are in gathering reliable information. With intimate knowledge of your adversary, you can employ flawless strategies to put a quick end to your conflict and restore peace.

Throughout these thirteen chapters, the protagonist is called "the general," which refers to a military leader—ancient or modern, Chinese or non-Chinese—who follows Sun Tzu's principles. As a general who followed these principles himself, Sun Tzu naturally used this language. But a "general" can also simply mean a leader. You don't have to be formally appointed to become a leader; you automatically become the de facto leader when you step up and guide others out of a dilemma and into a better situation. Therefore, your leadership ability depends more on your actions—your ability to apply The Art of War—than on your official title, rank, or station in life.

Any use of the masculine pronouns he or him for "the general" is only meant to illustrate, not to indicate a specific gender. The story of Hua Mulan—a first-century CE Chinese woman who illegally joined an all-male army but was later commended by the emperor for her martial ability and leadership—illustrates well that even in ancient China a woman with military skills was honored.

Above the Fray, You Have No Fear

> Though an army encamp against me,
> my heart shall not fear;
> though war rise up against me,
> yet I will be confident.
>
> (Psalm 27:3)

Understanding Sun Tzu's The Art of War enables you to live your life uninhibited by conflicts and intense competition. With mental rigor, you achieve peace not passively but with the utmost activity and diligence. This means not only being on the side of spirituality and benevolence but also on the side of shrewdness and preparedness. This way of living also recalls the kind-hearted but clear-eyed perspective Jesus encouraged his disciples to have in the midst of hardship and conflict, "Be wise as serpents and innocent as doves" (Matthew 10:16). Or as Henry David Thoreau, the famous nineteenth-century American naturalist and transcendentalist, refined it, "How often are we wise as serpents without being harmless as doves!"[10] Having both moral and intellectual superiority, you can end conflicts effortlessly within yourself and with others, and break down the barriers that too often separate you from what (or who) you truly value most in your life.

A Note on the Translation

During my early studies of Sun Tzu's The Art of War, one of the issues that concerned me the most was whether the English translation I was reading was accurately rendered from the original Chinese. In fact, this concern led me to obtain multiple editions to compare the similarities and differences between them and ascertain, as much as possible, what Sun Tzu's true intent was on a specific verse.

The main difficulty with The Art of War is that it was written so long ago. The Chinese language that Sun Tzu spoke and wrote on bamboo slips 2,500 years ago was vastly different from today's Chinese language. Even if you are fluent in modern Chinese, you would still have a very difficult time rendering the individual characters found in The Art of War. This is not unlike the struggle modern English speakers typically go through when trying to understand texts written in Old English "only" 1,250 years ago. Personally, I even have a difficult time understanding Shakespeare's English written just five hundred years ago without guidance.

There are a number of reasons why editions of The Art of War vary so widely, but two in particular are worth a closer look. First, translators sometimes define individual words too liberally and neglect to stay within the boundaries of the Chinese text itself. They rely too much on their own interpretation instead of respecting Sun Tzu's logic. Second, translators sometimes fail to seriously consider the context of the verses for verification and confirmation. By observing the context, the translator understands Sun Tzu's overall intent and can pinpoint a more exact meaning to a word that connects to the flow and theme of the section, chapter, and book.

Addressing the first problem, the editors of Sonshi.com and I started with a clean slate and translated each character with care, caution, and diligence from the original Chinese text. Without the rush of a deadline, we took the amount of time and effort necessary to see the project through properly. We stayed true to the Chinese characters themselves, painstakingly rendering them word by word in their own diction. What few additions we made (we made no deletions), were the result of nuances that required more English words to define, not our desire to express an idea that originated from our personal beliefs. In the end, the project took over a year to complete, representing countless hours poring through each character and debating what English word(s) best reflected its meaning. However, we didn't translate The Art of War in a vacuum. We referenced six previous editions of the book that were backed by decades of scholarship to substantiate our renderings. Complemented by the guidance and feedback of giants before us, we believe we have produced the ultimate edition.

Our confidence in the translation's accuracy rests on the scrutiny and meticulousness we gave to every Chinese character, such as *shih,* found in chapter 5, "Force." *Shih* is unstoppable power and momentum, yet that power and momentum are controlled and deliberate. This description is a mouthful, so our challenge was to mirror its Chinese form with the most fitting English word. We initially proposed a number of words, such as *power* or *influence*, but none seemed to depict it fully. So in this case we turned to the six selected editions and found the following translations: "strategic military power," "combat power," "energy" (twice), "strategic advantage," and "force." We all nodded our heads and unanimously agreed the best word was *force.* Interestingly, the edition that employed this translation was Thomas Cleary's. There are many connotations of force, such as brute force. But another kind of force is a latent, imperceptible, yet undeniable power that could only be fully harnessed and wielded by honorable individuals (not unlike the nature of the Force in the *Star Wars* movies). How appropriate for Sun Tzu and his The Art of War!

Addressing the second problem of translating Sun Tzu's words, we further established the appropriateness of every word or verse translation by determining its correlation to the context, both within the thrust of the immediate discussion and the overall The Art of War book.

For example, in chapter 3, "Planning Attacks," Sun Tzu writes about planning attacks and gaining overwhelming advantage, namely dividing the army:

> Generally in warfare:
>> If ten times the enemy's strength, surround them;
>> if five times, attack them;
>> *if double, divide them;*
>> if equal, be able to fight them;
>> if fewer, be able to evade them;
>> if weaker, be able to avoid them;
>> Therefore, a smaller army that is inflexible will be captured by a larger one.

For the italicized verse in this passage, we could depend on neither the Chinese character *fen* ("divide") to give us more clues (Divide who? Ourselves or our enemy?) nor previous works. The six editions were split on whether the general with twice the size of the enemy should divide the enemy's army into two or divide his own army into two.

However, once we reviewed the context, the answer soon became apparent. The core idea of this section of chapter 3, "Planning Attacks," is about achieving overwhelming strength in numbers, so much so that you can pressure the adversary to give up without having to resort to battle. You achieve this effect by surrounding him, as proposed by Sun Tzu, outnumbering him ten to one. Even with a five-to-one advantage you still have overwhelming strength and can secure victory. An army with a two-to-one advantage that divides itself is only of equal strength to its enemy. Engaging in battle with such odds is discouraged in chapter 10, "Ground Formation," where Sun Tzu says, "For expansive ground [where no one has advantage over the other], if the forces are equal, it will be difficult to do battle." But if the general divides *the enemy,* his army now outnumbers his opponent's four to one, very close to the five-to-one advantage that Sun Tzu advocates for attacking.

In addition, the only time Sun Tzu expressed numbers and dividing forces was when he talked about dividing the enemy's forces, not his own. Paralleling chapter 3, "Planning Attacks," the following verse in chapter 6, "Weakness and Strength," mentions the ten-to-one advantage: "If our army is at full force and the enemy is divided, then we will attack him at ten times his strength. Therefore, we are many and the enemy few. If we attack our many against his few, the enemy will be in dire straits." This enduring wisdom about remaining unified is reflected in Jesus's words, which were later paraphrased by Abraham Lincoln in reference to events that led to the American Civil War: "Every kingdom divided against itself is laid to waste, and no city or house divided against itself will stand" (Matthew 12:25).

In conclusion, take full advantage of our hard work and benefit from our translation's high level of accuracy and strict conformance to Sun Tzu's philosophy. To complete the translation, this book also has detailed explanations and annotations of all the important verses—unrivaled in depth and breadth by any edition of The Art of War available anywhere—to solidify your understanding. I envy you, because The Art of War—Spirituality for Conflict is an edition I wish I had had when I first started studying Sun Tzu's words twenty years ago. Yet I also have the fine pleasure to know that once you read this book, you will be empowered to further spread the message of wisdom and compassion, hope and peace to everyone you know—friends and enemies alike.

The Art of War—
Spirituality
for Conflict

◆ Calculation involves quiet deliberation, as in a temple, prior to taking action in warfare or in any conflict with opposing sides. When you encounter a conflict in your life, before you act, seek out a solitary place that balances and enhances your mind to spiritually think things through. For Sun Tzu, this process is more than merely collecting your thoughts. By intentionally reviewing five specific factors known as Way, Heaven, Ground, General, and Law, you can predict the outcome of any conflict even before making your first move.

1 In *Shih-chi* ("Historical Records"), China's first notable historian, Ssu-ma Ch'ien (145–ca. 86 BCE), recalled Sun Tzu explaining his military principles in both oral and written form to Ho Lu, king of the Wu state, in 512 BCE.

For over 2,500 years, many have found those principles relevant to their lives, and chances are good that by reading this book you will as well.

2 Sun Tzu highlights the destructiveness of war and thus the importance of studying and understanding it. Warfare means more than actual combat. It also encompasses social, economic, political, and even emotional aspects that influence and often determine the outcome of a military endeavor.

Although few of us will encounter warfare firsthand, we all experience conflicts in our lives. At home, you might argue with your spouse over a family matter. At work, you might contest a decision your boss has made. In other settings, you might encounter individuals who try to harm or discredit you for their own gain.

At times, you may try to avoid or gloss over the conflict because you don't want to deal with its difficult problems. But allowing a conflict to linger without resolution only exacerbates those problems. Avoiding or acquiescing to spiteful individuals, for instance, may temporarily eliminate discomfort, but will ultimately fuel your own resentment and may even incite suspicion of people in general.

So how do you go about resolving a conflict? According to Sun Tzu, you must first face the conflict and proactively seek to understand what lies at its root.

1 □ Calculations

Sun Tzu said:[1]

Warfare is a great matter to a nation;

it is the ground of death and of life;

it is the way of survival and of destruction, and must be examined.[2]

(continued on page 5)

3 If you want to prevail over your enemy or adversary, you need to determine—that is, make calculations—if you have superior strength over him or her in the five distinct factors: Way, Heaven, Ground, General, and Law.

♦ It is important that we define *enemy* or *adversary* before going further. An enemy or adversary is someone who seeks to do you harm. Although adversaries are always involved in conflicts, not all conflicts involve adversaries. You will sometimes find yourself in a conflict with non-adversaries, such as friends or family members who oppose you on a particular course of action, but whose motivations involve your best interests. In such cases, not all the strategies in this book will be appropriate, but if you can learn to peaceably resolve conflicts with your enemies, resolving conflicts with your loved ones will be even simpler.

This distinction is important because uninitiated readers might eagerly try to apply Sun Tzu's battle strategies on, for example, their own families—they would be misguided. You and your family no doubt have disagreements, but everyone works for the same goals, similar to how Sun Tzu and the people in his nation worked for the same goals. You don't want to subdue those you love and care about; you want to support them.

In The Art of War, Sun Tzu even advocates sacrificing his own welfare for his nation if that sacrifice means promoting the welfare of his people. In your personal life, you probably don't mind choosing to lose to your family in a conflict if you know they benefit. You would sacrifice your own well-being to ensure theirs.

4 The first of Sun Tzu's five factors is the Way or the Tao, which represents unity in a moral purpose. From top to bottom, people of all ranks strive for the same goal as if they are one person. The reason they unite lies in the morality of the goal: the greater the moral cause, the tighter the union. If your Way is strong, you will naturally garner strong support from others. With this support, you strengthen your position relative to your adversary's.

The fear of betrayal mentioned here is not the people betraying the leaders, but rather the leaders betraying the people by not acting in the people's best interest.

Therefore, go through it by means of five factors;

compare them by means of calculation, and determine their statuses:

one, Way; two, Heaven; three Ground; four, General; five, Law.[3]

The Way is what causes the people to have the same thinking as their superiors;

they may be given death, or they may be given life, but there is no fear of danger and betrayal.[4]

(continued on page 7)

5 The second of Sun Tzu's five factors is Heaven, which represents the atmosphere—the time of day, weather, and season. A soldier's abilities may depend on Heaven because night, bad weather, or the coldness of wintertime can prevent him or her from moving quickly and efficiently.

Heaven can likewise represent your social atmosphere—the moods and attitudes of those around you, which change over time yet repeat with regularity. Just as you cannot predict the weather with certainty, you cannot predict exactly when a person's mood and attitude will change and repeat. Nonetheless, you can anticipate these changes and benefit from them once they do occur. For example, you would be wise to ask for support from those around you when they feel hopeful, not fearful. Always be willing to assess if your environment is conducive to garnering the support you need to advance your cause.

6 The third of Sun Tzu's five factors is Ground, which represents the landscape, with its restrictions and freedoms. This factor weighs most on Sun Tzu's mind, and he devotes two entire chapters to Ground (chapters 10, "Ground Formation," and 11, "Nine Grounds"). He not only warns about the limitations of particular landscapes, but also points to the many possibilities various types of landscapes offer.

Ground represents many of the concrete factors that make up your environment, such as society's established laws or unwritten rules of acceptable social behavior. So although you cannot directly control the law or culture, and it often determines how you should approach your conflict, you do have the ability to choose when and where to take action based on your particular situation. For instance, you can formulate a strategy that is protected by the law or social norms; your enemy would be hard-pressed to oppose the legal system or draw society's disapproval of your actions. The endless patterns and configurations of Ground parallel the endless number of opportunities available to you to resolve your conflict.

Taken together, Heaven and Ground represent your overall environment. You can't substantially change or influence it, but if you are flexible and respond to each factor accordingly, you will create options that are advantageous for you.

Heaven is dark and light, cold and hot, and the seasonal constraints.[5]

Ground is high and low, far and near, obstructed and easy, wide and narrow, and dangerous and safe.[6]

(continued on page 9)

7 | The fourth of Sun Tzu's five factors is General, which represents five beneficial qualities of an effective leader. Without these five attributes, Sun Tzu believes the military general cannot earn the trust of his soldiers and, consequently, the full effort and commitment of his army. If you want to gain the full effort and commitment of those around you, you likewise must possess wisdom, credibility, benevolence, courage, and discipline. Wisdom is your good judgment. Credibility is your good reputation. Benevolence is your good intent. Courage is your good fortitude. Discipline is your good reliability.

In addition to the Way, the five attributes of wisdom, credibility, benevolence, courage, and discipline underscore that Sun Tzu wrote The Art of War from a moral perspective. Much like Jesus's observation that good trees cannot bear bad fruit (Matthew 7:18), the General's five attributes, if truly applied, cannot fulfill an evil purpose. Although Sun Tzu doesn't shrink away from promoting pragmatic means, as we will see, he insists that they will succeed only when motivated by these virtuous qualities.

8 | The fifth of Sun Tzu's five factors is Law, which represents the management of strength. To maintain their viability, large and complex organizations such as an army need a system to manage everyone's efforts and the proper and efficient allocation of resources. As can be found in any modern-day corporation, this system involves standard procedures, division of labor, procurement and distribution of materials, and cost reduction.

Sun Tzu also advises you to manage your strength by consistently conserving and restoring your energy. Take short bursts of action and long periods of practice and self-improvement. Don't chase after every petty matter and waste your energy. Organize and focus your efforts to continually build sufficient strength in order to quickly neutralize conflicts whenever they come your way. We will discuss this in more detail in chapter 2, "Doing Battle."

General is wisdom, credibility, benevolence, courage, and
  discipline.[7]

Law is organization, the chain of command, logistics, and the
  control of expenses.[8]

(continued on page 11)

9 In this verse, Sun Tzu implies that although all generals have heard of the five factors—Way, Heaven, Ground, General, and Law—some choose to ignore them. How unfortunate that these generals decided to ignore the factors even if doing so meant possibly averting hardship and bloodshed.

With knowledge comes responsibility; "from everyone to whom much has been given, much will be required" (Luke 12:48). Therefore, Sun Tzu urges you not only to read about the five factors but also to place them close to your heart. Since they affect the outcome of any conflict, you should examine, understand, and apply them.

10 Here Sun Tzu gives specific examples of how to calculate and compare the Way, Heaven, Ground, General, and Law between two sides. For the wise general, the real battle is fought here, in the quiet of the temple, before his army ever steps onto the battlefield. Implied in this verse is the need for your complete honesty and impartiality when determining the level of your strengths and your adversary's strengths in each of the five factors. This comparative examination isn't easy and may bruise your ego. But if you find you have a weakness, consider it a blessing because you can address the problem instead of remaining weak and unaware.

Once you have assessed all five factors you can formulate a strategy (an overall plan to reach your goal) and establish supporting tactics (the individual actions that support your strategy) to guide you to victory. Victory is achieved when you quickly end the conflict and regain harmony. Your conflict may be filled with emotion, but your plan to effectively resolve the conflict depends on logic and organization. With your bias-free deliberation of the five factors, you can prognosticate the outcome of the conflict before you ever lift a finger.

All these five no general has not heard;

one who knows them is victorious, one who does not know them is not victorious.[9]

Therefore, compare them by means of calculation, and determine their statuses.

Ask:

Which ruler has the Way,

which general has the ability,

which has gained Heaven and Ground,

which carried out Law and commands,

which army is strong,

which officers and soldiers are trained,

which reward and punish clearly,

by means of these, I know victory and defeat![10]

(continued on page 13)

| 11 | Backed by his vast knowledge and experience, Sun Tzu shows confidence in the effectiveness of his principles. From the late Spring and Autumn period (770–476 BCE) and into the Warring States period (475–221 BCE), Chinese military advisors were often hired and fired based on the results they individually produced, not their family relationship or background. This meritocracy summarily winnowed out the incompetent and gave rise to the best minds, whose sole job was to find ways to end warfare and resolve conflicts. This process of natural selection proves that the ideas Sun Tzu presents in The Art of War—ideas that enabled him to become one of the most successful generals of his era—truly work.

| 12 | Superiority in the five factors ensures victory, but how do you address contingencies—unexpected events or "outside missions"—that might upset your superior position *after* you take action? Through force. *Force* means having such overwhelming momentum that you can withstand setbacks. Force is the extra energy that helps you push through unforeseen situations and gives you the opportunity to create new advantages when necessary. Sun Tzu further discusses force in chapter 5, "Force."

| 13 | This famous verse is often quoted in the media or highlighted by people who take it out of context and suggest that The Art of War contains little more than devious techniques. After all, deception implies a dubious behavior that runs counter to ideals such as honesty and integrity. However, for Sun Tzu, deception in the service of a greater good is not devious, but rather a tool in the hands of a leader whose aim is noble. For example, deception allows you to remain "formless" so your adversary can't attack you. (The concept of formlessness is explored in chapter 6, "Weakness and Strength.") By thwarting an attack, you spare both you and your adversary the pain and hardship of battle. When you view deception in the light of saving lives and preserving resources, it can indeed serve a positive function.

A general who listens to my calculations, and uses them, will surely be victorious, keep him;

a general who does not listen to my calculations, and does not use them, will surely be defeated, remove him.[11]

Calculate advantages by means of what was heard, then create force in order to assist outside missions.

Force is the control of the balance of power, in accordance with advantages.[12]

Warfare is the Way of deception.[13]

(continued on page 15)

14 Sun Tzu gives specific examples of deception, which approach the opponent psychologically rather than physically, indirectly rather than directly. This perspective may seem contrary to the perceived physical and direct nature of warfare, where guns and bombs result in killing and destruction. However, when the enemy is confused and overwhelmed because of your deception, his or her will to continue fighting diminishes and the conflict is soon ended. Is this not the same result sought by using guns and bombs, but with less death and destruction?

Taoist sage Lao Tzu, who wrote the core Taoist text *Tao Te Ching*, said, "Those who are good at defeating enemies do not engage them." In other words, just because you can destroy your adversary doesn't mean you should. According to Sun Tzu, again highlighting his moral leaning, you should seek less aggressive and destructive means.

15 Due to deception's dependence on formlessness and the element of surprise, keep the action plan to yourself until the last moment.

16 Because battles in ancient China often involved hundreds of thousands of soldiers, they resulted in enormous loss of life and rapid depletion of valuable resources. Thus, a prudent military general such as Sun Tzu didn't wage war lightly or hastily. He needed time away in the temple to deliberate on the five factors of Way, Heaven, Ground, General, and Law, and to determine which side had the advantage.

How many times in your life could you have abated conflicts if you had taken the time to deliberate on your problems in quiet contemplation—for example, taking a quiet walk—to think about your capabilities and limitations, and the likely gains and losses of taking action? By removing yourself from the immediate, stressful situation, you also take out the emotion that often prompts you to make rash, thoughtless decisions. The temple, whether real or proverbial, lifts you above the fray and enables you to see the world for what it likely is, instead of what you want it to be. It is no wonder that Buddha believed detachment and serenity went hand in hand (and that only with both could compassion emerge).

Therefore, if able, appear unable;

if active, appear not active;

if near, appear far;

if far, appear near.

If they have advantage, entice them;

if they are confused, take them;

if they are substantial, prepare for them;

if they are strong, avoid them;

if they are angry, disturb them;

if they are humble, make them haughty;

if they are relaxed, toil them;

if they are united, separate them.

Attack where they are not prepared, go out to where they do not expect.[14]

This specialized warfare leads to victory, and may not be transmitted beforehand.[15]

Before doing battle, in the temple one calculates and will win, because many calculations were made;

before doing battle, in the temple one calculates and will not win, because few calculations were made;

many calculations, victory, few calculations, no victory, then how much less so when no calculations?

By means of these, I can observe them, beholding victory or defeat![16]

◆ According to Sun Tzu, a skillful military general only does battle when there is no other option. Many disagreements can be solved without the situation escalating into actual confrontation or battle, which often exacts a heavy toll on both sides. Even when your adversary is an aggressor bent on fighting you, you can still seize the initiative and win without fighting if you obtain a superior mental, physical, and moral position according to the five factors explored in chapter 1. This is true whether the opposing side is an army, a nation, or an individual. However, if you conclude that doing battle is inevitable, following Sun Tzu's principles in this chapter will ensure a quick victory with minimum suffering.

1 Sun Tzu looks at the big picture. He begins his discussion of doing battle not with details of tactics or weapons, but by outlining the great costs involved in joining battle. Carefully calculating the cost of confrontation with your adversary is one way to ensure you don't rush recklessly into the conflict. Notice that Sun Tzu lists no cavalry. During his lifetime (544–496 BCE), horses were used only in conjunction with the chariot because the Chinese didn't yet have saddles or stirrups.

2 In Sun Tzu's time, a *li* was approximately 400 meters or a quarter of a mile. Thus, the one thousand *li* mentioned in this verse equals approximately 250 miles.

Although Sun Tzu doesn't say so explicitly, the guests he refers to are friends, allies, and advisors from outside the state who can provide the military leader information on the enemy's plan, condition, or location. Gathering such pertinent information helps circumvent hardship and waste because the general then knows exactly where best to employ his soldiers and resources. We will discuss this topic in more detail in chapter 13, "Using Spies." In that chapter, Sun Tzu notes the costs associated with having these guests, but it is relatively low in comparison with the invaluable function they serve to help reduce the loss of lives and the time and effort needed to prepare for battle—and even sometimes to prevent battles altogether.

2 □ Doing Battle

Sun Tzu said:

Generally, the requirements of warfare are this way:

One thousand quick four-horse chariots,

one thousand leather rideable chariots,[1]

one hundred thousand belted armor,

transporting provisions one thousand *li*,

the distribution of internal and on-the-field spending,

the efforts of having guests,[2]

(*continued on page 19*)

3 Cataloging these expenses is Sun Tzu's way of asking: Are you willing to expend your valuable resources and have an iron commitment to do battle? If you aren't, then consider other options. Half measures mean half effort, which can result in failure. The expense of properly setting in motion a military campaign is staggering, but the true cost is even greater when you account for the lost opportunities to build and improve instead of preparing for battle. Therefore, before making the decision to go to battle, you must be certain that it is your only choice.

4 If the general must engage his enemy in battle because there is no other option, he wants to settle it quickly not only to limit the costs, but also to prevent exhaustion or loss of morale among his troops. Sun Tzu was pragmatic in this assessment. He understood what we today often forget: heated political rhetoric can get a nation into a war, but when the words and emotion fade away and the conflict drags on, the nation grows weary of the economic and human toll of war, and wants out.

When tension erupts into conflict in your own life, the sooner you address and resolve it, the sooner you can mend your relationship with your opponent and get on with your life. A disagreement that lingers unresolved is fuel for a grudge, which can turn into a feud, which benefits no one.

You can end conflicts quickly by having a clear idea of what you want to accomplish and then focusing all your efforts on accomplishing it. To ensure you don't waste time and prolong the conflict, take only those actions that help, and refuse to take actions that don't help. Your time is limited, as are your energy and resources. You are better off being frugal with all three.

materials such as glue and lacquer,

tributes in chariots and armor,

will amount to expenses of a thousand gold pieces a day.

Only then can one hundred thousand troops be raised.[3]

When doing battle, seek a quick victory.

A protracted battle will blunt weapons and dampen ardor.

If troops lay siege to a walled city, their strength will be exhausted.

If the army is exposed to a prolonged campaign, the nation's resources will not suffice.[4]

(continued on page 21)

5 If the general pours all of his energy into fighting one enemy over an extended period of time, his army won't have any strength left to be sufficiently prepared to deal with other enemies when they emerge. Therefore, Sun Tzu warns against exhausting your energy on one adversary as if he or she is the only person in the world who can harm you. It's possible that other individuals are simply waiting for the ideal moment and conditions to attack you. Whether you'll handle this problem calmly or frantically depends on your readiness. As you'll later learn in chapter 8, "Nine Changes": "Do not depend on the enemy not coming, but depend on your readiness against him."

6 If the general fails to prepare for battle before he hears of the enemy advancing, his chances of survival are slim. No amount of wisdom can reverse the inevitable when a demoralized and exhausted army without resources is attacked by a well-prepared, opportunistic neighbor. Even if you prefer to not do battle, you should always be alert to the possibility that battle will be forced on you by conserving your energy and resources to maintain readiness.

For Sun Tzu, wisdom is proactive, not reactive. Wisdom opens your mind to the most viable options given your specific situation and enables you to act appropriately to help avert dire situations. However, once pressed into a corner with no viable option, even the wise may find that it is too late.

7 Those who prolong the fight instead of trying to abate it may be motivated by an unhealthy desire to win at any cost. This impulse may find expression in a nation's military activities or in a minor disagreement where neither party is willing to concede. Even though Sun Tzu would likely agree that persistence is a positive trait, here he qualifies it by pointing out its negative side, perhaps better described as stubbornness. The desired result is the end of warfare—victory—not the subjugation of the enemy after many long and costly battles. An imaginary nation with infinite resources might be able to wage war relentlessly with little trouble, but in the real world, prolonged warfare leads to defeat or, at best, a Pyrrhic victory.

When weapons are blunted and ardor dampened, strength exhausted and resources depleted, the neighboring rulers will take advantage of these complications.[5]

Then even the wisest of counsels would not be able to avert the consequences that must ensue.[6]

Therefore, I have heard of military campaigns that were clumsy but swift, but I have never seen military campaigns that were skilled but protracted.

No nation has ever benefited from protracted warfare.

Therefore, if one is not fully cognizant of the dangers inherent in doing battle, one cannot fully know the benefits of doing battle.[7]

(continued on page 23)

8 | Sun Tzu shows his pragmatism by proposing that an army feed itself from the bounty of the enemy's land, thereby bypassing the costly need to transport basic supplies from far away. Skillful leaders ensure a quick victory, rendering unnecessary the need to raise fresh troops and provide additional supplies.

Before you decide to take action and confront your adversary, consider whether you would exhaust your energy and resources before you gain victory. You might determine that you will need to depend on your adversary to sustain your progression. Examples of such resourcefulness include using your enemy's best ideas, skills, technologies, and people (by befriending and enlisting the aid of her supporters, for example) to help your cause.

9 | The "citizens' wealth" used to launch a military campaign refers to the wealth of the citizens back home. When a nation needs to raise taxes to extend a war—leaving the poor, who have the least to give, with the biggest burden— it signifies desperation more than an intelligent approach to conflict.

Although Sun Tzu advocates feeding off the enemy's land and army, he doesn't believe in plundering the enemy's citizens. Sun Tzu once again reveals his morality by factoring in the high cost of purchasing (not taking) food and supplies from the enemy's citizens, even in time of war. Implied in this verse then is safety for his enemy's civilians, which was advocated 2,500 years later in the Fourth Geneva Convention of 1949.

Besides being morally sound, Sun Tzu's approach is also entirely practical. Whatever enemy land and resources that remain intact are the general's gain. (This preference for keeping his enemy whole instead of destroying it is further explored in chapter 3, "Planning Attacks.") Moreover, granting civilians and their property safety and respect helps defuse tensions and create goodwill—or at least lessen ill-will—on the part of the region's inhabitants. When General Robert E. Lee led his Army of Northern Virginia into Maryland in September 1862 during the American Civil War, he issued strict orders that his Confederate troops pay for anything they took from the Yankee civilians. By contrast, the Union army in pursuit of Lee was notorious for looting the countryside and even its own citizens.

Those skilled in doing battle do not raise troops twice, or transport provisions three times.

Take equipment from home but take provisions from the enemy.

Then the army will be sufficient in both equipment and provisions.

A nation can be impoverished by the army when it has to supply the army at great distances.

When provisions are transported at a great distances, the citizens will be impoverished.[8]

Those in proximity to the army will sell goods at high prices.

When goods are expensive, the citizens' wealth will be exhausted.

When their wealth is exhausted, the peasantry will be afflicted with increased taxes.[9]

(continued on page 25)

[10] Sun Tzu again emphasizes the waste and overall adverse effect on society when the army exhausts massive amounts of wealth and materials in lengthy military campaigns. If you think Sun Tzu exaggerates the high cost of war, or that things are different today, consider this: According to the Stockholm International Peace Research Institute (SIPRI), the world currently spends $1.2 trillion a year on the military, an amount equal to the entire annual gross domestic product of Canada, America's largest trading partner! Imagine if that money was instead invested in education, medicine, housing, or the environment—areas that sustain and improve society instead of having the potential to destroy it. The true cost of war, in terms of money spent as well as opportunities lost, is utterly staggering.

Sun Tzu's warning about the inevitably wasteful nature of war extends to conflicts in your own life. Judicious preparation for conflicts is necessary, but becoming obsessed or paranoid consumes your time, energy, and resources, all of which could be conserved for contingencies or used on other pressing matters.

Notice the fractions of seven-tenths and six-tenths, which represent the spent citizens' wealth and army's reserves after a campaign. What little remains would be insufficient to send more troops, equipment, and provisions a second time, which explains the necessity of feeding off the enemy and seeking the quick victory.

[11] We can infer from this verse that in Sun Tzu's time it cost twenty pounds of food to transport one pound of food. Whether Sun Tzu used the twenty-to-one ratio literally or poetically, the costly decision to use only your own resources instead of also relying on your adversary's is clear. With modern technology, the cost of logistics has gone down, but the concept of loss and waste remains.

When all strength has been exhausted and resources depleted, all houses in the central plains utterly impoverished, seven-tenths of the citizens' wealth dissipated,

the government's expenses from damaged chariots, worn-out horses, armor, helmets, arrows and crossbows, halberds and shields, draft oxen, and heavy supply wagons,

will be six-tenths of its reserves.[10]

Therefore, a wise general will strive to feed off the enemy.

One bushel of the enemy's provisions is worth twenty of our own, one *picul* of fodder is worth twenty of our own.[11]

(continued on page 27)

[12] Sun Tzu here reveals a keen eye for human psychology and what motivates people. Though he recognizes the motivational power of anger, which destroys, he instead appeals to reward and benevolence, which build up. Specifically, his counsel is to commend and encourage your own best soldiers and to treat prisoners kindly so that they will want to join your own ranks. This simultaneously reduces the enemy's strength and increases your own. Treating the enemy soldiers with kindness is yet another example of how Sun Tzu wisely balances the practicality and ruthlessness of war with morality and compassion.

You can follow this approach in your own life. When you have a superior position against your adversary's relatively weak state, you can offer an olive branch and signal your benevolent intentions by treating him or her well. Now you have a better chance of disarming your adversary without further fighting. A passage attributed to Lao Tzu states, "Because you do not contend so the world cannot contend with you." In other words, if you choose not to fight, your foe is less likely to choose aggression. Both sides can stop wasting energy and resources; both sides can benefit. The goal, as always, is to achieve a quick and decisive victory, which limits the suffering of everyone involved.

[13] Sun Tzu reiterates his belief that wars don't enhance security, but rather weaken it by sowing the seeds of future conflicts. Thus, the skillful general doesn't simply win battles—he prevents them when possible. When prevention is not possible, he achieves victory quickly. Hence, he is the guardian of people's lives, not just because he defeated the enemy, but because he preserved the lives and security of the nation.

If your adversary tries to do you harm, your aim is not mere retaliation, but a quick resolution. Use your superior strength not to cause more hardship and suffering, which results in his or her enduring hatred of you, but to promote harmony and forgiveness through sincere gestures of goodwill. These acts will go much further toward a lasting peace than simply defeating your adversary, who may harbor a grudge and reignite the conflict later.

Killing the enemy is a matter of arousing anger in men;

taking the enemy's wealth is a matter of reward.

Therefore, in chariot battles, reward the first to capture at least ten chariots.

Replace the enemy's flags and standards with our own.

Mix the captured chariots with our own, treat the captured soldiers well.

This is called defeating the enemy and increasing our strength.[12]

Therefore, the important thing in doing battle is victory, not protracted warfare.

Therefore, a general who understands warfare is the guardian of people's lives, and the ruler of the nation's security.[13]

◆ When battle is inevitable, the best way to achieve a swift victory is to craft a careful plan. This stops waste, preserves resources, and may possibly earn you the goodwill of your adversary. Planning attacks includes taking decisive action—but it also includes deliberate and timely *in*action. In this chapter Sun Tzu also presents another set of five factors that determines whether you'll succeed in your conflict.

1 With no sign of vengeance or retaliation in his heart, Sun Tzu aims for preservation and humaneness even in the midst of the violence of war. You may be surprised to see this call for compassion in a book called The Art of War, but there is a practical side to being compassionate. Little good comes from a decimated city and its embittered population. The general would want that city standing and its population supportive of his army. No wonder Lao Tzu said, "So when evenly matched armies meet [where none has numerical advantage], the side that is compassionate shall win."

Sun Tzu here challenges the notion many of us have that in order to win, you must *beat* your competition. Causing your adversary unnecessary suffering doesn't make your own situation any better. In fact, it might harm your position because it incites his or her hatred of you. Once you put aside emotional cries for vengeance and retaliation, as did Sun Tzu, you are able to start making decisions impartially and will discover that you can improve your own strength and position without ruining your adversary.

2 From the national level down to the level of an individual squad, the principle remains the same: the art of war ("best") is preserving an enemy; the artless practice of war ("second best") is destroying your opposition. What may take a nation decades to build and nurture can be destroyed in an instant. What was once a unique fellow human being, albeit an enemy, can become an unidentifiable corpse. Destruction is relatively easy; creating and preserving—to maximize your gains and empathize with your adversary—require time and effort that few people may want to take.

3 □ Planning Attacks

Sun Tzu said:

Generally in warfare, keeping a nation intact is best, destroying a nation, second best;[1]

keeping an army intact is best, destroying an army, second best;

keeping a battalion intact is best, destroying a battalion, second best;

keeping a company intact is best, destroying a company, second best;

keeping a squad intact is best, destroying a squad, second best.[2]

(continued on page 31)

3 Winning one hundred times in one hundred battles requires amazing skill and intelligence, but winning one hundred times without fighting a single time demonstrates maturity and compassion as well. Sun Tzu sees that even if a general won an incredible one hundred battles, the heavy costs of engaging in those battles was a bitter price to pay. Sun Tzu certainly values winning, but not at any cost. So what better way to avoid the costs of fighting than by winning without fighting?

There is irony in this. When you attain the "highest of excellence" by achieving victory without a fight, very few people will take notice. You remain anonymous or may even be disparaged. But when you attain a lesser excellence of winning one hundred battles, with their attendant waste and destruction, people will heap praise on you. Therefore, true excellence manifests from the objective evaluation of yourself and not necessarily from what other people think of you. The writer of Ecclesiastes in the Hebrew Bible makes a similar poignant observation:

> I have also seen this example of wisdom under the sun, and it seemed important to me. There was a little city with few people in it. A great king came against it and besieged it, building great siegeworks against it. Now there was found in it a poor, wise man, and he by his wisdom delivered the city. Yet no one remembered that poor man. So I said, "Wisdom is better than might; yet the poor man's wisdom is despised, and his words are not heeded."
>
> (Ecclesiastes 9:13–16)

Therefore, to gain a hundred victories in a hundred battles is not the highest excellence;

to subjugate the enemy's army without doing battle is the highest of excellence.[3]

(continued on page 33)

4 In 500 BCE China, Hantan, the capital city of Chou, had walls measuring sixty-five feet thick and fifty feet high. In an age with no artillery and only rudimentary siege contraptions, you can imagine the arduous effort necessary to take over such a major city.

In this verse, the progression from most desirable to least desirable focus of attack is inversely proportional to the amount of physical damage an army can inflict on its enemy: the less damage inflicted, the more desirable the outcome. (This is perhaps counterintuitive, until you remember the value Sun Tzu places on compassion.) Another consideration implied in this verse is how early the general addresses the enemy: the earlier he takes action, the less amount of damage he can do and still win—and therefore the more desirable the victory.

In everyday situations, it is best to address conflicts as early as possible, and to focus on your adversary's actions or behaviors (the enemy's "plan") that are external to his identity, not attack head-on his personality (the enemy "army") or core beliefs. Such diplomacy minimizes damage to his ego, and, because he will not perceive your attack as a personal affront, you will much more easily get what you want—the cessation of the objectionable behavior.

5 In order to scale fifty-foot city walls, a Chinese general needed a tremendous amount of time and effort for preparation. If he wasn't patient and sent in his men immediately hoping for quicker results, many would die in vain.

When you face a seemingly insurmountable obstacle—a metaphorical fifty-foot wall—you might be tempted to launch a hasty, all-out assault on it. But such an approach is futile and only wastes your energy and resources. Instead, Sun Tzu advises that you approach the problem patiently. Break it down into component parts and solve each one in succession. In interpersonal conflicts, try mending smaller fences, finding common ground where it does exist. In this way, you will experience less stress, expend less of your energy and resources, and still make steady, consistent progress.

Therefore, the best warfare strategy is to attack the enemy's plans, next is to attack alliances, next is to attack the army, and the worst is to attack a walled city.

Laying siege to a city is only done when other options are not available.[4]

To build large protective shields, armored wagons, and make ready the necessary arms and equipment will require at least three months.

To build earthen mounds against the walls will require another three months.

If the general cannot control his temper and sends troops to swarm the walls, one third of them will be killed, and the city will still not be taken.

This is the kind of calamity when laying siege to a walled city.[5]

(continued on page 35)

6 This is Sun Tzu's reminder not to settle for what's most expedient, but to pursue the best solution, which is a peaceful solution. When you take the time and effort to do what's right and not just what's easy, you'll see the difference in the permanency of your success.

7 People in ancient China believed that heaven, earth, and humankind are interconnected. The direct link between heaven and humankind was the emperor, who, although thought to be wise and benevolent, was legitimized only by the Mandate of Heaven, which demanded that he exude virtue by taking care of his people—indeed, All-Under-Heaven. If he did not, he would be replaced by another emperor who would. This belief explained for the Chinese the succession of dynasties; over time, as each dynasty became corrupt, it was usurped by another more in line with heaven's virtue.

Sun Tzu simply extends this concept to military leaders. Much like the people's unity with their ruler, the soldiers' unity with their general depends on the uprightness of the general. This concept perfectly defines the Way or the Tao discussed in chapter 1.

8 Besides following the Mandate of Heaven to keep All-Under-Heaven intact, there is a more practical, down-to-earth reason to minimize destruction: the less that is destroyed, the less energy and resources you have to expend restoring the military, infrastructure, and culture. In the everyday conflicts you face, your gains may spring from relationships you manage to keep intact despite being in conflict with them. With no words or deeds to regret, you can confidently move on with your life.

Therefore, one who is skilled in warfare principles subdues the enemy without doing battle, takes the enemy's walled city without attacking, and overthrows the enemy quickly, without protracted warfare.[6]

His aim must be to take All-Under-Heaven intact.[7]

Therefore, weapons will not be blunted, and gains will be intact.[8]

These are the principles of planning attacks.

(continued on page 37)

9 If he has a ten-to-one advantage, a general knows he can display such overwhelming strength that the opposition will have no choice but to give up. Staying true to the principle of winning without fighting, even with a lopsided advantage where he can easily crush his enemy, a wise general aims instead to surround the enemy, thereby dramatically proving the futility of continuing the fight. He thus not only has a good chance of winning without bloodshed, but also may gain the trust and respect of the opposing side.

You can go beyond your basic instinct to destroy or show aggression or arrogance when you're in a superior position. You can show your kindness and view it as giving you more strength, not less. Working in tandem with your superior position, kindness further leverages your influence on your opponent by weighing heavily upon his or her mind, emotion, and logic, thus achieving victory without actual confrontation.

10 Sun Tzu's humanity again shows through here. He doesn't mobilize the army and risk people's lives unless he knows from deliberation that he can prevail. He advocates attacking only when he has reached a five-to-one advantage, which isn't as visually and mentally overwhelming as ten-to-one but is still sufficient to quickly settle the fight if he must do battle.

Notice that when the odds are even, one to one, Sun Tzu says, "Be able to fight them," not, "Fight them." Because he is merely equal with his enemy, he wouldn't actively seek battle. But if he is forced to fight, he needs to be able to fight—not for gain in this case, but for survival.

An unwise person, who is motivated by emotion more than deliberation, seeks direct confrontation even when he or she is weaker. But to Sun Tzu, there is no shame or cowardice in avoiding battle if you decide, after careful consideration of the situation, that it will avert a disastrous outcome. Therefore, your success in resolving many conflicts—especially those for which you are unprepared—depends more on your *not* taking action than taking action. Only move if you know you will benefit from making that move; otherwise, your energy is best used to improve yourself and build strength.

Generally in warfare:

If ten times the enemy's strength, surround them;[9]

if five times, attack them;

if double, divide them;

if equal, be able to fight them;

if fewer, be able to evade them;

if weaker, be able to avoid them.

Therefore, a smaller army that is inflexible will be captured by a larger one.[10]

(continued on page 39)

11 Through his civic duties the Chinese emperor governed the people, but the military general protected them from the harmful effect of conflicts with other nations. Even today, if a general fails at his job, the nation is in peril and subject to constant fear. If he succeeds at his job, however, then the nation is safe and secure enough to concentrate on improving itself and building its strength. As if aware an entire population depends on him, a wise general realizes his responsibilities transcend his own personal concerns. This, in turn, gives him the motivation and inner strength to do his job well.

Despite the problems that concern you in your everyday duties, realizing that your responsibility is larger than yourself motivates you to give your best no matter what the task. There is no room for pettiness, arrogance, or fear to take root. If you think about other people and how your actions affect them, you will prevail ethically in your conflicts and ordeals.

12 A ruler in ancient China had immeasurable power and influence over his people, more so than any president or prime minister today. Able to summarily kill or pardon anyone, he was accountable to no one but heaven; he was the personification of divinity and was obeyed without question. The military general worked for the ruler and swore allegiance to him. Nevertheless, Sun Tzu candidly argues that an uninformed ruler meddling in the affairs of the army could put the nation at risk. That the general pledges loyalty to the ruler doesn't mean he must always obey the ruler. His loyalty is deeper: it lies in protecting the well-being of the ruler and nation, not in blindly following orders.

Sun Tzu would likewise advise you to think for yourself and not blindly acquiesce to the demands of others. In small matters, you might go with the flow, but in an important matter that undermines your well-being and the well-being of others around you, you must have fortitude to rely on your own critical thinking.

A general is the safeguard of the nation.

When this support is in place, the nation will certainly be strong.

When this support is not in place, the nation will certainly not be strong.[11]

There are three ways the ruler can bring difficulty to the army:

To order an advance when not realizing the army is in no position to advance, or to order a withdrawal when not realizing the army is in no position to withdraw.

This is called entangling the army.

By not knowing the army's matters, and administering the army the same as administering civil matters, the officers and troops will be confused.

By not knowing the army's calculations, and taking command of the army, the officers and troops will be hesitant.[12]

(continued on page 41)

13 Near the end of the Spring and Autumn period in China, numerous states vied for survival and increased their power by incorporating surrounding weak states into their own. Thus, each state kept a close eye on who was vulnerable for attack.

If you have superior knowledge of a situation yet acquiesce to the advice of others, you have made yourself weaker all on your own, without the involvement of your adversary. Rendering adversaries harmless is tough enough—why make yourself your own worst enemy?

14 The five factors mentioned here are different from the Way, Heaven, Ground, General, and Law discussed in chapter 1. These new factors are more narrowly defined and give you another angle for finding victory in your conflicts.

The first of the five factors is knowing when to take action and when not to take action. What prevents you from knowing when to fight and when not to fight is not caution but arrogance. Caution at times forestalls you from taking rash action. Arrogance, on the other hand, overstates your abilities and advantages and incorrectly encourages you to move forward with an unworkable plan. To avoid acting in arrogance, you must contemplate your situation while in a quiet place. Your deliberateness allows you to visualize the consequences of your actions—before you take action—and thus helps you to determine when you can fight and prevail, and when you cannot.

15 The second of the five factors is knowing how to manage people. Sun Tzu believes that if the general has a way to organize and communicate effectively to each and every soldier, he can lead them to victory, no matter the size of his army.

The inspiring message you give to one person that motivates him or her to support your cause will likely motivate numerous others to support your cause. Regardless of the size of your audience, if your message comes straight from your heart, you will speak with the same tone and inflection, motivating them all just the same because you appeal to each individual on a personal level.

When the army is confused and hesitant, the neighboring rulers will take advantage.

This is called a confused and hesitant army leading another to victory.[13]

Therefore, there are five factors of knowing who will win:

One who knows when he can fight, and when he cannot fight, will be victorious;[14]

one who knows how to use both large and small forces will be victorious;[15]

(continued on page 43)

16 The third of the five factors is creating unity within the army. This is analogous to cultivating the Way, where both the leader and the people share a single purpose. You unite people by finding and emphasizing what everyone has in common, not what makes him or her different. In a large group, the diversity of skills and perspectives is invaluable in identifying creative solutions to a complex problem, but this diversity means little if it isn't focused on one problem, a common cause.

17 The fourth of the five factors is preparation. According to Sun Tzu, a prepared army is a strong army, whereas an unprepared army is a weak army. This relates to the element of time. An army becomes strong when it takes the time to prepare its attack. An army becomes weak when it doesn't have enough time to prepare against an attack.

18 The fifth of the five factors is competence and the confidence to stand up to superiors. The general has the moral obligation and responsibility to take the best course in spite of what others who have less knowledge think. He keeps his promise to protect the well-being of his nation and do what is right for the long-term instead of choosing what is expedient for the short-term. If the correct decision means the lives of thousands of his men, he has good reason to be resolute.

Sun Tzu emphasizes the need to have confidence in yourself. If you have direct knowledge, don't waver against those who have less knowledge. Ambivalence helps no one, including you. As the New Testament notes, "A double minded man is unstable in all his ways" (James 1:8 KJV). To succeed in your life's conflicts, you cannot be unstable but must have conviction in your beliefs, even when they differ from those of your adversaries or even your superiors. Your ability to gently persuade the other side, either through logic or appeal to their self-interests, could result in a quick victory without confrontation.

one who knows how to unite upper and lower ranks in purpose will be victorious;[16]

one who is prepared and waits for the unprepared will be victorious;[17]

one whose general is able and is not interfered with by the ruler will be victorious.[18]

These five factors are the way to know who will win.

(*continued on page 45*)

19 This verse is perhaps The Art of War's most quoted in the modern media to illustrate the cause behind a war's failure. All too often, when a conflict flares up, your focus is on yourself—either protecting your own interests or acting emotionally to seek vengeance or retaliation. Both of these motivations are liable to lead to defeat because they leave little time and effort for a deeper understanding of the broader and complete view of your situation, specifically the many perspectives influencing that situation.

Acting unilaterally out of emotion or self-interest, paradoxically, works against your own best interests. Sun Tzu disdains such an approach as foolish and deeply misinformed. Instead, he proposes that you study all aspects of a problem coolly and rationally, plan carefully, and act prudently while trying to minimize damage. This means that sometimes active inaction will be the best course until circumstances change and you have the advantage necessary to prevail.

Therefore I say:

One who knows the enemy and knows himself will not be in danger in a hundred battles.

One who does not know the enemy but knows himself will sometimes win, sometimes lose.

One who does not know the enemy and does not know himself will be in danger in every battle.[19]

◆ Formation means more than simply the physical position you take to face your adversary; to Sun Tzu, it is the position of invincibility your adversary cannot surmount. This state of invincibility reduces the number of conflicts you will have to face, because adversaries will quickly see the futility of trying to challenge you. If an adversary does try to start a confrontation with you, you can successfully defend yourself with ease. You cannot fail because you only confront those who are already defeated. In this chapter you will also learn how to consistently gain victory by resolving problems while they are still minor, thus preventing them from growing into unwieldy or intractable challenges that require actual confrontation to resolve.

1 Sun Tzu starts this verse with "in ancient times" to indicate the timeless value of thorough preparation. If an army is thoroughly prepared, it needs only to wait patiently for its enemy to display a vulnerability, and then strike. Your ability to secure your formation of invincibility begins with you alone. Through preparation you gain invincibility, which ensures your safety. This invincibility gives you time to patiently choose the right moment to take action so you can ethically and methodically settle conflicts with even those of malevolent intent.

2 The army can be invincible, but this doesn't mean it can conquer another army that is also invincible. Sun Tzu cautions against arrogance here. Even though you may have the knowledge and experience to plan and employ the best strategy, your adversary may be strong and cunning enough to block off that strategy. Thus, regardless of your strength, success is never guaranteed. Believing you will always prevail can lead to waste and possibly catastrophe. From this verse you can infer that you should neither overestimate your own strength nor underestimate the strength of your opponent. If you aren't stronger than your adversary, then you wait. If you are stronger than your adversary, then you can take action. Whatever the situation, you can't unilaterally control it, so you must adapt to it.

4 □ Formation

Sun Tzu said:

In ancient times, those skilled in warfare make themselves invincible and then wait for the enemy to become vulnerable.

Being invincible depends on oneself, but the enemy becoming vulnerable depends on himself.[1]

Therefore, those skilled in warfare can make themselves invincible, but cannot necessarily cause the enemy to be vulnerable.

Therefore it is said one may know how to win but cannot necessarily do it.[2]

(continued on page 49)

47

3 The difference between defending and attacking is your level of focus and strength. When you defend, you can focus on one area you have built sufficient strength to protect. You therefore can achieve invincibility. However, when you attack, you also still need to defend yourself. Your focus is now split into two activities, and in order to do both effectively, you require more strength. If your strength remains fixed, attacking takes focus away from your defense and leaves you vulnerable.

4 In Chinese lore, dragons hid in the lowest depths of the earth when dormant, which was most of the time. Yet when they roused themselves and rose into the sky, they were incredibly powerful and fearsome. This latent strength represents invincibility well. The army spends most of its time resting, training, and building strength within the confines of its encampment. But when the army decides to move and become visible to the enemy, it moves with ferocious power and alarming quickness.

When you conceal yourself from view, no one knows how strong you are or where to attack. During this uninterrupted period, you can practice and prepare yourself before you take action. Once you take action and show yourself, you must move swiftly and with full force so you are always one step ahead of your adversary. Therefore, in order to quickly solve your life's problems, such as conflicts, don't settle for half-hearted efforts; once you make up your mind to accomplish a mission, you must complete it without hesitation.

5 Just as it does not take refined senses to perceive the sun or moon, or great strength to lift the fine down of a rabbit's autumn coat, so it takes comparatively less skill to resolve problems once they flare into open conflicts. True skill and wisdom lie in the ability to perceive slight variations in your environment and in your adversary in order to nip problems in the bud before they become obvious and damaging.

One takes on invincibility defending, one takes on vulnerability attacking.

One takes on sufficiency defending, one takes on deficiency attacking.[3]

Those skilled in defense conceal themselves in the lowest depths of the Earth, Those skilled in attack move in the highest reaches of the Heavens.

Therefore, they are able to protect themselves and achieve complete victory.[4]

Perceiving a victory when it is perceived by all is not the highest excellence.

Winning battles such that the whole world says "excellent" is not the highest excellence.

For lifting an autumn down is not considered great strength, seeing the sun and the moon is not considered a sign of sharp vision, hearing thunder is not considered a sign of sensitive hearing.[5]

(continued on page 51)

6 Soldiers can't show their bravery if they don't have a chance to fight. Generals can't prove their wisdom in battle strategy if they never wage war. Generals and soldiers can't display their skills if their enemy is easy to conquer. However, Sun Tzu questions the relevance of accolades in warfare. He reminds us here that what should be forefront in our mind is victory, not ego or reward.

Sometimes, achieving an "easy" victory actually requires special skill. For example, you might use diplomacy to successfully negotiate with someone who is angry. However, if you had greater skill, you would perceive that person's irritability and work to defuse it before it turns into anger. When you tackle basic matters such as this, you will be unlikely to miscalculate as you would in more complex and advanced matters. Your success in small conflicts would therefore appear to be simple, but in reality it requires a special heightened sensitivity to your environment and adversary.

7 Croesus, king of Lydia, (595–ca. 546 BCE) was the richest man of his time, but was warned by Solon, a Greek legislator, on how luck played a large part in his fortune and that it all could soon evaporate if he took further unmitigated risks. Later, having lost a battle to Persian king Cyrus, Croesus was about to be killed when he shouted, "Solon, you were right!" Cyrus inquired why he shouted this, and after Croesus explained, Cyrus spared his life knowing full well that his own fortune could turn, too. Therefore, understand the role played by luck in your past successes and in your life—mistaking good fortune for skill could cause you to act recklessly and put you in danger in the future.

8 "Governing victory and defeat" implies having the ability to pick and choose between the two. Similar to how a prudent general avoids stronger armies and engages only weaker ones, you can govern your success in conflicts by only confronting adversaries you can handle and avoiding those you cannot. This avoidance is not the same as avoiding the conflict itself. Don't ignore the problem; face it and study it, then select your path accordingly.

In ancient times, those who were skilled in warfare gained victory where victory was easily gained.

Therefore, the victories from those skilled in warfare are not considered of great wisdom or courage, because their victories have no miscalculations.

No miscalculations mean the victories are certain, achieving victory over those who have already lost.[6]

Therefore, those skilled in warfare establish positions that make them invincible and do not miss opportunities to attack the enemy.

Therefore, a victorious army first obtains conditions for victory, then seeks to do battle.

A defeated army first seeks to do battle, then obtains conditions for victory.[7]

Those skilled in warfare cultivate the Way and preserve the Law; therefore, they govern victory and defeat.[8]

(continued on page 53)

9 Sun Tzu outlines a logical framework for determining who will emerge victorious in a conflict:

Ground is your environment, or where you are. (For example, the culture in which you live.)

From Ground, you can then measure the freedoms and constraints the environment gives both you and your adversary. (What are the values of that culture—what is prized and what is despised?)

From what you measured in freedoms and constraints, you can then quantify your and your adversary's respective advantages and disadvantages. (What attributes do you and your opponent have that are prized or despised in that culture?)

From what you quantified in advantages and disadvantages, you can then calculate the strengths and weaknesses in yourself and your adversary. (Which of those attributes would give you and your opponent influence? Which would incite scorn?)

From what you calculated in strengths and weaknesses, you can then compare those strengths and weaknesses to determine which side has superiority. (Of those attributes that give you influence, do you have more of them than your opponent? Of those attributes that incite scorn, do you have fewer of them than your opponent?)

From your comparison to determine which side has superiority, you can then predict which side will likely achieve victory. (Comparing yourself to your opponent, who ultimately would draw more influence and less scorn?)

The factors in warfare are:

First, measurement; second, quantity; third, calculation; fourth, comparison; and fifth, victory.

Measurements are derived from Ground,

quantities are derived from measurement,

calculations are derived from quantities,

comparisons are derived from calculations,

and victories are derived from comparisons.[9]

(continued on page 55)

10 Here Sun Tzu uses two vivid metaphors to describe the army's invincible formation or position. A properly formed army is like a ton crushing an ounce, or like deep waters released and raging through a gorge. In either case, it is unstoppable.

You should seek a position that gives you such an overwhelming advantage over your adversary that he or she will not try to confront you because doing so would be hopeless. In this way, you achieve the highest excellence by stopping conflicts before they even start—this is winning without fighting. Because conflict is prevented, your true level of sensitivity and skill may go overlooked, but no one can deny the peace that you bring to those around you.

A victorious army is like a ton against an ounce;

a defeated army is like an ounce against a ton!

The victorious army is like pent-up waters released, bursting
through a deep gorge.

This is formation.[10]

♦ Once you establish an invincible position, or formation, you can proceed to employ force, which is action taken with overwhelming momentum. You create force by organizing and concentrating all your energy and resources toward a single effort, and mixing what Sun Tzu called "common" and "uncommon" ways to disrupt your adversary and change the balance of power. Then, with precise timing and undeniable strength against your adversary's weak point, you can overwhelm him or her and end the conflict quickly.

1 Sun Tzu's first lesson on force is control. The army's momentum alone is useless or even harmful if the general cannot control it. You see uncontrollable power in chaotic situations such as a mass riot. By contrast, an effective general controls force when he aligns his soldiers' energies and unites them by directly communicating with them through his officers, flags, and pennants. He might not be present, but the message is delivered to every solider as though he were. Therefore, whether his army consists of one thousand men or one hundred thousand, he still can unite it and maintain control.

If you can unite ten people to support you in your effort, you likewise can unite one thousand; it is simply a matter of communicating the same message to many more people. However, this unity can only be accomplished if you can achieve the Way, uniting everyone in and believing in the moral integrity of your purpose. This begins with your own conviction, for if you are not convinced of the righteousness of your own cause, how can you plausibly convince others to follow you? Sun Tzu advises you to achieve harmony and balance with yourself and those close to you first. Only then can you hope to effectively achieve harmony with potential supporters and even adversaries.

5 □ Force

Sun Tzu said:

Generally, commanding of many is like commanding of a few.

It is a matter of dividing them into groups.

Doing battle with a large army is like doing battle with a small army.

It is a matter of communications through flags and pennants.[1]

(continued on page 59)

2 One way of controlling your force is through two distinct types of maneuvers or movements, here called "common" and "uncommon." For the general, common maneuvers are the normal, textbook movements he takes to first engage the enemy army. Uncommon maneuvers are the radical, unexpected movements he takes to upset the balance of power during the battle and, hopefully, deliver the final blow to the enemy. For example, the army can attack the enemy directly at the front in a common maneuver, but flank him at the side in an uncommon maneuver.

The nuance here is that what is an uncommon maneuver in one circumstance can be a common maneuver in another, depending on the adversary's expectations. For example, if the enemy is *expecting* a flanking maneuver, then that becomes the common maneuver and the frontal assault is the uncommon move that will take him by surprise. In this way the two categories of common and uncommon maneuvers, through a judicious use of strategy, tactics, timing, and psychology, yield an endless array of possible ways you can move your force to swiftly overcome your opponent.

Sun Tzu's vivid image of a stone thrown against an egg represents an uncommon maneuver applied effectively against a surprised and unprepared enemy. Such a surprise action is one way to create force in your situation.

3 Like the general, you can start with common ways to try to end your conflict. If that doesn't work, try uncommon ways. Fortunately, there are so many potential uncommon approaches to your problem that you are limited only by your imagination. With so many possibilities, you will encounter very few conflicts you can't resolve in some satisfactory manner.

4 In this verse, *they* refers to common and uncommon maneuvers. Sun Tzu points out why, just as the sun and the moon and the four seasons change and rotate, common and uncommon maneuvers must also continually change and rotate: to gain an advantage by surprising your opponent and catching him or her off-guard.

What enables an army to withstand the enemy's attack and not be defeated are uncommon and common maneuvers.

The army will be like throwing a stone against an egg;

it is a matter of weakness and strength.[2]

Generally, in battle, use the common to engage the enemy and the uncommon to gain victory.

Those skilled at uncommon maneuvers are as endless as the heavens and earth, and as inexhaustible as the rivers and seas.[3]

Like the sun and the moon, they set and rise again.

Like the four seasons, they pass and return again.[4]

(continued on page 61)

5 Just as the finite number of five notes, colors, and flavors can become infinite once they combine, so too can common and uncommon maneuvers when combined. If your adversary expects the ordinary, employ the extraordinary. If your adversary expects the extraordinary, employ the ordinary. With so many possible combinations, how can your adversary prepare for them all?

In China's folklore, the number five symbolizes universal concepts, such as the five elements (earth, metal, wood, fire, water) and five directions (center, west, east, south, north). To the ancient Chinese, the finite five elements and directions encapsulate everything and everyplace—the infinite universe—so it is understandable why Sun Tzu references the number five to explain the many combinations resulting from just two types of maneuvers. (Notice that you are now on the fifth chapter, in the fifth annotation.)

6 The uncommon maneuver cannot be extraordinary without the common maneuver first being ordinary, much like the summer season cannot become summer without being preceded by spring. This understanding is right at home in Taoist thinking—you cannot have "good" if you do not also have "bad," and vice versa. Each gives birth to the other. In this way, a careful use of combined common and uncommon maneuvers will disorient the enemy: as if examining a circle, the opposition does not know when a common maneuver starts and when an uncommon maneuver ends.

There are no more than five musical notes, yet the variations in the five notes cannot all be heard.

There are no more than five basic colors, yet the variations in the five colors cannot all be seen.

There are no more than five basic flavors, yet the variations in the five flavors cannot all be tasted.

In battle, there are no more than two types of attacks:

Uncommon and common, yet the variations of the uncommon and common cannot all be comprehended.[5]

The uncommon and the common produce each other, like an endless circle.

Who can comprehend them?[6]

(continued on page 63)

7 Another way to create force is to intentionally channel all your energy and resources in one overarching effort. Sun Tzu uses five metaphors to illustrate the concept of force: a stone thrown at an egg, massive rushing waters, a bird of prey's strike, a drawn crossbow, and (later in the chapter) logs or boulders rolling down a mountain. In a more modern example, you might view a speeding locomotive as a picture of force. In all cases, you can visualize an unstoppable power moving in a single direction that will achieve some inevitable end—in your case, victory.

Victory and momentum work in concert with each other. When you start to win, you become motivated, which brings forth more energy. This cycle creates yet more momentum, which in turn brings you additional victories. In this way, winning feeds itself. Timing remains a crucial component of force, however—momentum can turn to chaos if it is not focused on a particular goal at the precise, opportune time. But with overwhelming force and precise timing, victory is all but assured.

8 This verse can be confusing. How can courage create fear, strength create weakness, and order create disorder? These have to do with a general's skill in effectively implementing uncommon maneuvers, which depend on deception. He cannot feign fear without first having courage, feign weakness without first having strength, feign disorder without first having order. To display an advantage is common, but feigning a disadvantage in order to lure the enemy into a vulnerable position is uncommon and catches the adversary off-guard, changing the balance of power in the general's favor.

When you're in the midst of a chaotic situation, do you have the mental stability to remain calm? With formation, where you have a position of invincibility and feel no fear of danger, you can. However, to catch your adversary unprepared and subdue him, you may also need to employ uncommon methods, such as feigning fear despite your lack of it. Don't use deception for the sake of deception, but to render your adversary harmless.

The rush of torrential waters tossing boulders illustrates force.

The strike of a bird of prey breaking the body of its target illustrates timing.

Therefore, the force of those skilled in warfare is overwhelming, and their timing precise.

Their force is like a drawn crossbow and their timing is like the release of the trigger.[7]

Even in the midst of the turbulence of battle, the fighting seemingly chaotic, they are not confused.

Even in the midst of the turmoil of battle, the troops seemingly going around in circles, they cannot be defeated.

Disorder came from order, fear came from courage, weakness came from strength.

Disorder coming from order is a matter of organization, fear coming from courage is a matter of force, weakness coming from strength is a matter of formation.[8]

(continued on page 65)

9 The true formation here is still one of invincibility, but the one displayed is one of vulnerability. This is feigned "weakness coming from strength"—bait that entices the enemy to overextend himself. Because the adversary is the aggressor, he is either angry or greedy and so is blind to the trap. He will be caught off balance and his weaknesses will be exposed, allowing you to pacify him and immediately put an end to the confrontation.

The reason you won't fall for this same trap when employed by others is your moral compass and noble intentions. You do not attack out of angry or selfish motives, but rather to stop the conflict out of benevolence. As the Taoist master Lao Tzu proclaimed, "In using the military, there is a saying: I dare not be the host [the attacker], but prefer to be the guest [the defender]. I dare not advance an inch, but prefer to withdraw a foot."

10 This verse is Sun Tzu's way of saying that no matter how little skill a person possesses, he or she can still serve a needed function and contribute to the force of the organization. Conversely, no matter how much skill one person possesses, he or she isn't critical in the grand scheme.

11 The force of a trained, prepared, and united army is like a large round log or boulder waiting to be released downhill. Once the general releases the army, it becomes unstoppable. Even if one soldier wants to stop, he cannot because the entire army sweeps him along.

You can create force by first gathering the support of those around you and uniting everyone's effort in a single cause. This mass of support represents the round logs and boulders. However, in order to start their momentum at the right time, you need a way to communicate with them directly. This communication represents the releasing of the logs or boulders. Mixing common and uncommon methods, as if they are in an endless cycle, changes the balance of power and accumulates momentum until you're unstoppable against your adversary, like a log or boulder rolling down a steep mountain; this is force.

Therefore, those skilled in moving the enemy use formation to which the enemy must respond.

They offer bait that the enemy must take, manipulating the enemy to move while they wait in ambush.[9]

Those skilled in warfare seek victory through force and do not require too much from individuals.

Therefore, they are able to select the right men and exploit force.[10]

One who exploits force commands men into battle like rolling logs and boulders.

Logs and boulders are still when on flat ground, but roll when on steep ground.

Square shapes are still, but round shapes roll.

Therefore, those skilled in warfare use force where the troops in battle are like boulders rolling down a steep mountain.

This is force.[11]

♦ Until now, Sun Tzu has generally addressed situations where you are more powerful than your adversaries. But what if they have more power than you? In this chapter Sun Tzu explicitly discusses how you can negate your weaknesses and accentuate your strengths, thereby rendering your enemies harmless—even if they are more powerful. You do this by becoming formless, a position that prevents them from determining where you are vulnerable, while allowing you to uncover their positions of strength and weakness. With this advantage in knowledge, you can avoid your adversaries' strengths, surprise them by applying all your force to their weakest point, and overcome them.

1 Sun Tzu observes that an army at full strength and positioned on advantageous landscape occupies a supremely enviable position. An enemy that comes against such a stronghold must be motivated by emotion—such as anger or greed—rather than wisdom, and soon finds that his attack will become drained of its energy. Thus, though it remains unmoved, the army can use the enemy's rash behavior against him.

Even before a confrontation starts, you can gain an immediate advantage by becoming like a majestic mountain that moves for no one. With a calm, serene mind, you conserve your energy while your adversary, motivated by frenetic emotions, will soon exhaust himself as he comes against you. This serenity is the same principle behind the ancient art of tai chi. Although it is widely seen as a slow, meditative exercise, tai chi was first developed as a martial art designed to allow your adversary's own unbalanced mind and body to become the source of his own defeat.

2 Since your adversary is guided by emotion, you can manipulate him into moving at your will. If you show a threat, his fear and shortsightedness will cause him to pause. If you motivate him with easy gain, he will gravitate toward it. Ironically, you use his negative energy to guide him further away from harming you.

6 □ Weakness and Strength

Sun Tzu said:

Generally, the one who first occupies the battlefield awaiting the enemy is at ease;

the one who comes later and rushes into battle is fatigued.

Therefore, those skilled in warfare move the enemy, and are not moved by the enemy.[1]

Getting the enemy to approach on his own accord is a matter of showing him advantage;

stopping him from approaching is a matter of showing him harm.[2]

(continued on page 69)

3 In addition to maximizing your own position and strength, Sun Tzu here outlines ways to further reduce your enemy's strength. This double effort helps you to further increase the disparity between your position and your adversary's, empowering you to end the conflict swiftly and decisively.

Sun Tzu's admonition in this case, as always, is to remember that your primary goal should be to use your lopsided advantage not to ruin or even subdue your enemy, but to convince him or her of the futility of fighting in the first place, and hence avoid unnecessary suffering for everyone involved.

4 As mentioned in chapter 2, one thousand *li* is approximately 250 miles.

Even if the opposition is stronger, the consummate general can still create advantages. Instead of engaging his enemy in battle in every encounter, he reconnoiters where the enemy is strong and avoids it. Thus the general not only conserves energy and resources from not having to fight, but also moves with ease and peace of mind no matter how far the distance. He would rather travel long distances on a safe road than travel a short distance on a perilous road. In short, a general maintains the safety of his army by avoiding the enemy's strong areas, and ensures the army's success by attacking the enemy's weak areas.

In your everyday conflicts, instead of tackling the risky issues your adversary would strongly oppose, choose to first address safer issues on which both sides have some agreement. As you steadily overcome your differences with your opponent, opportunities may open and new understandings spring forth where you can then overcome an issue that before seemed impossible to reconcile.

Therefore, if the enemy is at ease, be able to exhaust him;

if the enemy is well fed, be able to starve him;

if the enemy is settled, be able to move him;

appear at places where he must rush to defend, and rush to places where he least expects.[3]

To march over a thousand *li* without becoming distressed, march over where the enemy is not present.

To be certain to take what you attack, attack where the enemy cannot defend.

To be certain of safety when defending, defend where the enemy cannot attack.[4]

(continued on page 71)

5 Sun Tzu explains that becoming formless means concealing your actual strengths and weaknesses. This doesn't mean, however, that you necessarily hide yourself physically from your adversary like a ninja or Marine sniper. Working out your problems with her in the open will not pose a threat, for if your true strengths and weaknesses are imperceptible, how will she know where best to attack or defend—even if you are standing face to face? Your cloak of mystery and subtlety hides your weaknesses. It also accentuates your strengths, for your adversary is likely to overstate the actual threat you pose when she is in such an unbalanced and uninformed position. In this way, achieving formlessness enables to you maintain force and influence, and you can pressure your adversary into a resolution that is in your favor.

6 When you see opportunities to put a quick end to your conflict, take immediate action. Similarly, when confronted with an impossible situation, withdraw immediately. This rushing is different than your adversary's haste as discussed in the first verse—your actions are swift and decisive, the result of clear vision and a calm mind. Your adversary's rash actions are the result of clouded vision and a mind ruled by emotion.

Therefore, against those skilled in attack, the enemy does not know where to defend;

against those skilled in defense, the enemy does not know where to attack.

Subtle! Subtle!

They become formless.

Mysterious! Mysterious!

They become soundless.

Therefore, they are the masters of the enemy's fate.[5]

To achieve an advance that cannot be hampered, rush to his weak points.

To achieve a withdrawal that cannot be pursued, depart with superior speed.[6]

(continued on page 73)

7 The military general can prompt a stubborn enemy to move if he attacks what his enemy values, an indirect approach that will lure the opposition out of his invincible position. Similarly, if a powerful enemy threatens the general's army, attacking elsewhere on what the enemy values will effectively draw off the enemy's attack and divert his attention elsewhere. In both scenarios, the general doesn't idly wait to see what the enemy does but proactively influence his opponent's movements.

Sun Tzu advises you to not take a passive role, waiting until opportunities magically present themselves, but rather to engage in an active, dynamic modus operandi that controls the tempo and direction of the present moment. For example, if your adversaries stubbornly stick to one position, identify what they cherish most and then deliberately seize or brandish it. This action gives them compelling incentive to change their position.

8 The importance of formlessness cannot be emphasized enough. With formlessness, even a weak army can subdue a strong one. Formlessness allows you maximum flexibility without diminishing your power. Because your strengths and weaknesses are a mystery to your adversary, he must divide his forces and resources, while you remain at full strength. This gives you the ability to attack any number of his vulnerable spots at will with your full force, which will now have the effect of a vastly larger force than you actually have.

Therefore, if we want to do battle, even if the enemy is protected by high walls and deep moats, he cannot but do battle, because we attack what he must rescue.

If we do not want to do battle, even if we merely draw a line on the ground, he will not do battle, because we divert his movements.[7]

Therefore, if we can make the enemy show his position while we are formless, we will be at full force while the enemy is divided.

If our army is at full force and the enemy is divided, then we will attack him at ten times his strength.[8]

(continued on page 75)

9 The "few" and "many" in this verse refer to the quantities you employ at a particular place and time, not your overall strength. With formlessness, you can remain centered in your own abilities and act wisely, which optimizes your effective strength when and where you choose to act.

10 Sun Tzu recaps here why the army must remain formless. Because the number of soldiers and resources are finite and he does not know where the battle will begin, the enemy, in his hope to cover all his bases, must defend in many places. But by doing so, he spreads himself thin and becomes vulnerable.

This principle was dramatically demonstrated in World War II by Operation Fortitude South, a bold plan of deception that masked the Allies' true intentions regarding the D-day invasions of Europe. By remaining formless, the Allies forced the Axis powers to divide their forces to meet several possible threats, instead of concentrating their forces at Normandy in northern France, where the invasion successfully landed on June 6, 1944.

11 Sun Tzu further explains why the act of defending everywhere will, paradoxically, leave you vulnerable everywhere. Even his tone effectively mimics a frantic defensive mode. When you rush to defend and merely survive, your adversary will know you don't have sufficient strength to defend yourself and don't know what to do. On the other hand, when you calmly and proactively seek to control the tempo of the conflict, you demonstrate competency and strength to your adversary.

12 Knowledge, more than actual strength, dictates the general's effectiveness in battle. With knowledge, he acts confidently, swiftly, in unison with all his forces, and with the ability to be compassionate. Without knowledge, he becomes scattered, vulnerable, fearful, and focused merely on trying to survive.

Therefore, we are many and the enemy few.

If we attack our many against his few, the enemy will be in dire straits.[9]

The place of battle must not be made known to the enemy.

If it is not known, then the enemy must prepare to defend many places.

If he prepares to defend many places, then the forces will be few in number.[10]

Therefore, if he prepares to defend the front, the back will be weak.

If he prepares to defend the back, the front will be weak.

If he prepares to defend the left, the right will be weak.

If he prepares to defend the right, the left will be weak.

If he prepares to defend everywhere, everywhere will be weak.

The few are those preparing to defend against others, the many are those who make others prepare to defend against them.[11]

Therefore, if one knows the place of battle and the day of battle, he can march a thousand *li* and do battle.

If one does not know the place of battle and the day of battle, then his left cannot aid his right, and his right cannot aid his left;

his front cannot aid his back, and his back cannot aid his front.

How much less so if he is separated by tens of *li*, or even a few *li*.[12]

(continued on page 77)

[13] Sun Tzu believes superior size and numbers by themselves don't always translate into fundamental strength or universal advantage. How you optimize your resources and allocate them determines whether you have strength or advantage.

Yueh, mentioned in this verse, was a southern Chinese state and was the neighboring enemy of Wu, Sun Tzu's state. Despite Yueh's superior manpower, the weaker Wu won the majority of the battles. The Yueh generals apparently depended more on their numerical strength than on their strategy to limit human losses. It wasn't until 473 BCE, well after Sun Tzu's death, that Yueh managed to conquer Wu, but it was then, in turn, defeated by a rejuvenated Ch'u state. Yueh's willingness to suffer casualties continued into modern history: the name *Viet Nam* means "south of the Yueh," and some Chinese scholars consider the Vietnamese to be descendants of the Yueh.

[14] In battle, a wise general determines his enemy's true strength or weakness by testing and observing the enemy's reaction to the bait. If the enemy reacts with overwhelming force, he is likely strong. If the enemy doesn't take the bait with voracity, he is likely weak. If the enemy's reactions are consistent after several tests and observances, the general has confidence in pinpointing his enemy's exact strength or weakness.

At times it may appear impossible to ascertain your adversaries' strengths and weaknesses. Like you, they try to become formless. However, you can still tease out information. For instance, you can determine how strongly your adversaries feel about an issue by proposing it and gauging their reactions for or against it. According to Sun Tzu, the best indicator of your opponents' true position is not through their words but through their past and present actions.

You can also use this method to reveal the true character of individuals you don't know. Observe how they act under stress or when they are given more power. Do they react to stress and power with wisdom and compassion or do they descend to fear and selfishness?

Based on my calculations, though Yueh's troops were many, what advantage was this to them in respect to victory?

Therefore I say, victory can be achieved.

Though the enemy is many, he can be prevented from doing battle.[13]

Therefore, know the enemy's plans and calculate his strengths and weaknesses.

Provoke him, to know his patterns of movement.

Determine his position, to know the ground of death and of life.

Probe him, to know where he is strong and where he is weak.[14]

(continued on page 79)

15 Sun Tzu recognizes the supreme skill necessary to obtain formlessness. The verse suggests that Sun Tzu prefers formlessness over superior size because no matter how strong you are, your adversaries can still find your weak points. If formless, you can remain whole and strong in your adversaries' mind even if you are actually divided and weak. Sun Tzu also explains that formlessness requires humility. Making a show of power might make you feel more secure, but in reality it only serves to advertise your weaknesses to your adversaries.

16 Formation is the position of invincibility you take against your enemies (see chapter 4). The key lesson Sun Tzu offers is that this formation is not fixed, but is flexible according to the enemy you face and the environment you are in. Much like selecting the right tool to repair a particular machine, you must select the right approach for the particular adversary you face. Your adversaries all possess different degrees of strength and weakness and hold different advantages and disadvantages.

Those who study your past strategies see how you overcame your conflicts, but rarely do they dig deeper to understand the principles behind why those strategies work. Emulation only works if the circumstances stay the same, but they usually do not.

This is why The Art of War continues to have relevance in our modern world despite its great antiquity. The genius of this work lies in the core principles that transcend time and place—and even warfare itself. Methods of waging war have evolved over the centuries to meet new kinds of challenges, and because The Art of War's core principles rest not on specific strategies but rather on issues that account for human nature, it has remained remarkably flexible and powerfully relevant across centuries and continents.

The ultimate skill is to take up a position where you are formless.

If you are formless, the most penetrating spies will not be able to discern you, or the wisest counsels will not be able to do calculations against you.[15]

With formation, the army achieves victories yet they do not understand how.

Everyone knows the formation by which you achieved victory, yet no one knows the formations by which you were able to create victory.

Therefore, your strategy for victories in battle is not repetitious, and your formations in response to the enemy are endless.[16]

(continued on page 81)

17 Water, a common Taoist symbol, is an appropriate metaphor for adapting to your situation and choosing the right formation in relation to your adversary's strengths and weaknesses. Like water rushing through a gorge and engulfing its unique rocky features, you rout attacking enemies by concentrating your force at their weakest, lowest point, where they can resist the least.

18 Whatever was effective in the past may be ineffective in the present or future. Nothing remains constant, so new circumstances deserve new approaches. This is as true of shifting conditions on the battlefield as it is of the seasons of your life.

Understanding this principle helps you to see that even long-standing and entrenched conflict can be changed with innovative, humane thinking. In war-torn feudal Japan during the Muromachi period (1338–1573 CE), warlords Uesugi Kenshin and Takeda Shingen, both practitioners of Sun Tzu's The Art of War, were bitter enemies. On one occasion, another warlord cut off Shingen's supply of salt, a precious commodity used to preserve food. After hearing of Shingen's predicament, Kenshin sent Shingen's province a large supply of salt and wrote him a letter declaring the salt blockade cruel and unjustified. Kenshin set the example for acting humanely toward the enemy, and though historical records show that the two remained opposed to each other, they thenceforth treated each other with respect and dignity.

You can employ similar creative, compassionate approaches when facing your adversaries. Combat anger with kindness; combat greed with generosity. Whether you convert them to friends or they remain adversaries, seek to change the tone of your conflicts, as Kenshin did, by minimizing your differences and creating new opportunities to more easily resolve those differences.

The army's formation is like water.

The water's formation avoids the high and rushes to the low.

So an army's formation avoids the strong and rushes to the weak.

Water's formation adapts to the ground when flowing.

So then an army's formation adapts to the enemy to achieve victory.[17]

Therefore, an army does not have constant force, or have constant formation.

Those who are able to adapt and change in accord with the enemy and achieve victory are called divine.

Therefore, of the five elements, none a constant victor, of the four seasons, none has constant position;

the sun has short and long spans, and the moon waxes and wanes.[18]

◆ Despite your best efforts, you will not always be able to prevent conflict, and so at times you must proactively engage with your adversary. In military terms, armed struggle is the hardship an army experiences as it moves over distances to execute the general's strategy. This differs from what is discussed in chapter 6, where the goal is to have the adversary come to you; here, you go to him should the need arise. Fortunately, as this chapter explains, there are ways to do this and still conserve your energy and obtain advantage over your adversary.

1 The military general, after receiving his orders, promptly prepares for battle. This responsibility isn't an easy one since it involves a multitude of people doing a multitude of tasks properly and in a timely way before the first soldier can step onto the battlefield.

This verse also touches on the necessity of someone overseeing your movements—not to ensure that you blindly follow orders, but to hold you accountable for your actions and performance. In your everyday life, you likely have someone who holds you accountable, and likewise hold others accountable. Sun Tzu was in a similar position, supporting both his superiors and subordinates, and The Art of War reflects a keen understanding of the challenge of this combined role.

2 The army mobilizes and executes the general's strategies in armed struggle. Given the context of this verse, "the circuitous" is not simply the long route but the traditional route. "The direct" is the quicker or shortened route that gives the army advantage over its opposition. Because soldiers often experience hardship as they march through circuitous routes, the general's duty is to improve their speed, lessen their hardship, and conserve their energy by making those routes more direct.

As you sometimes struggle through your day, you may want to pause and see if your usual behavior and habits contribute to your hardship. With calm determination, you can set forth to change or improve your behavior and habits and thus transform your struggle into opportunity.

7 □ Armed Struggle

Sun Tzu said:

Generally, the principles of warfare are:

The general receives his commands from the ruler, assembles the troops, mobilizes the army, and sets up camp.[1]

There is nothing more difficult than armed struggle.

In armed struggle, the difficulty is turning the circuitous into the direct, and turning adversity into advantage.[2]

(continued on page 85)

3 By baiting the enemy with easy gain, the general can divert him from his intended course and distract him from focusing on what's really important. The general's army can then continue on ahead and secure a favorable position before the enemy does.

4 Every decision carries with it risks that must be carefully weighed. If you want to gain an advantage in speed and progress, you must reduce your support and thus risk your safety. If you want to ensure safety and retain your resource advantage, you must settle for slower progress.

Similarly, most decisions in your everyday life require some kind of risk or trade-off, and your challenge is to find the optimal balance that you can live with. For example, many people struggle with spending time in the workplace versus time with their families—they often feel like they are sacrificing one for the other.

5 This is an illustration of how risking safety for superior speed can cause the general trouble because he doesn't have the protection he needs. "Rolling up" a soldier's armor is to bundle it and leave it behind with the other equipment and supplies to lighten the load and increase speed.

Therefore, if you make the enemy's route circuitous and bait him with advantages, though you start out behind him, you will arrive before him.

This is to know the calculations of the circuitous and of the direct.[3]

Therefore, armed struggle has advantages, and armed struggle has risks.

If the entire army mobilizes for an advantage, you will not arrive on time.

If a reduced army mobilizes for an advantage, your stores and equipment will be lost.[4]

For this reason, by rolling up your armor, rushing forward without stopping day or night, covering twice the usual distance for an advantage a hundred *li* away, the general will be captured.[5]

(continued on page 87)

6 The farther the army's destination, the thinner its resources are stretched, and the smaller its chances of success. The general may be the only person capable of formulating a sound strategy, but the success of the strategy's execution depends on the entire army. As gifted and strong as some extraordinary individuals are, they cannot produce the desired result without the support of many people behind them. The more difficult the goal, the more support leaders will need. If you arrive first but without the full support you need, your efforts will have been in vain.

7 Sun Tzu reaffirms your need to possess sufficient strength at all times, hedging your risk against unexpected attacks from powerful adversaries and other unforeseen dangers.

8 Sun Tzu describes a way to advance with speed and full strength— by gaining and using specialized knowledge that helps you find reliable shortcuts and avoid unnecessary risks. With this knowledge, you can make perilous roads safe and crooked paths straight. This is the best of both worlds. Speed means moving fast, but moving fast without knowing where you are going only gets you lost faster. So, in the context of The Art of War, speed means reaching your goals before your adversaries, not simply going faster.

As you expand your intellectual and physical horizons and want to be effective, you need to depend on the capabilities of other people. We all have areas where we are knowledgeable and areas where we are ignorant. When you find yourself in unfamiliar territory, seek counsel and ask for help. For example, if you regularly stay after hours at your workplace, identify your skill deficiencies and enlist the assistance of others so you can complete your tasks sooner and spend more time with your family. Struggling toward a difficult goal by yourself may be futile, but with help, even the impossible is within reach. Proverbs 24:5–6 states this paradigm clearly:

Wise warriors are mightier than strong ones,
and those who have knowledge than those who have strength;
for by wise guidance you can wage your war,
and in abundance of counselors there is victory.

The strong will arrive first, the weak will lag behind, and as a rule, only one-tenth will arrive.

If one struggles for an advantage fifty *li* away, the general of the front forces will be thwarted, and as a rule only one-half will arrive.[6]

If one struggles for an advantage thirty *li* away, then two-thirds of the army will arrive.

For this reason, if an army is without its equipment, it will lose;

if an army is without its provisions, it will lose;

if the army is without its stores, it will lose.[7]

Therefore, one who does not know the intentions of the rulers of the neighboring states cannot secure alliances.

One who does not know the mountains and forests, gorges and defiles, swamps and wetlands cannot advance the army.

One who does not use local guides cannot take advantage of the ground.[8]

(continued on page 89)

9 | Here Sun Tzu summarizes concepts of deception and adaptability introduced in previous chapters. Deception helps you to achieve formlessness so adversaries cannot ascertain your strengths and weaknesses to do you harm. When you apply your strength against the adversaries' weaknesses, you have an advantage similar to a stone against an egg. Such overwhelming force is controlled by close communication with those around you, which allows them to change with you when you adapt to the situation. You remain relevant and effective because the process of change itself helps you to remain formless to your adversaries.

10 | Sun Tzu was as much a poet as he was a warrior. His vivid metaphors evoke powerful, sublime images drawn from the natural world. What in our world has more force than these natural phenomena? Even our most impressive technologies and accomplishments pale in comparison.

Advancing like the wind means advancing nimbly and without interruption. Wind can go through or around obstacles and cannot be blocked. Marching like the forest means proceeding in orderly unison and in great numbers. Invading and plundering like fire means sweeping through with such intensity that few adversaries dare challenge you. Standing like a mountain means establishing unmovable resolve and principle. You may bend with the situation but you don't compromise on your purpose and integrity. Being formless like the dark means concealing your strengths and weaknesses so your adversaries cannot make calculations against you. Striking like thunder means exuding such overwhelming force that your adversaries respect you, and thus you have influence over them.

Therefore, the army is established on deception, mobilized by advantage, and changed through dividing up and consolidating the troops.[9]

Therefore, it advances like the wind;

it marches like the forest;

it invades and plunders like fire;

it stands like the mountain;

it is formless like the dark;

it strikes like thunder.[10]

(continued on page 91)

11 As discussed in chapter 2, annotation 9, this plundering applies to the enemy's land and army, not its citizens. According to Sun Tzu, whatever gain you obtain from your adversaries should be shared with those who helped you. By taking selfishness out of your decision making, you solidify trust among your people and allies. Ego is entirely missing in Sun Tzu—none of the actions he advocates are for personal advancement or glory or wealth. They are for a noble purpose.

When you show such a noble purpose in your everyday actions, you give people ample reason to support you. With their continued support—a strong foundation—you are able to hold on to your gains and be shielded from loss. Your progress is like climbing a ladder, a simple advance straight up without fear of backsliding or losing your footing.

12 Sun Tzu adds another key element of succeeding in armed struggle: communication. In ancient China, the general communicated his commands to the soldiers by way of drums, gongs, flags, and pennants. Sun Tzu started chapter 5 discussing why commanding many is similar to commanding a few—it is simply a matter of communication. Without an effective method to disseminate your message and make yourself understood, you cannot work in concert with anyone, whether you are commanding thousands of soldiers or talking with your spouse.

Very little is known about the Book of Military Administration referenced in this verse other than the obvious, that it is an "old book on war." Interestingly, Sun Tzu cites the Book of Military Administration as the authority, but it has long been forgotten, while Sun Tzu's own book has survived down through the ages. This demonstrates The Art of War's usefulness to many readers throughout history—even to the extent that some carried it to their graves. In 1972 at Silver Sparrow Mountain in China's Shantung province, archaeologists uncovered a second-century BCE tomb of a high-ranking Chinese official. Buried with him was a copy of The Art of War—the earliest known copy in existence today.

When you plunder the countryside, divide the wealth among your troops;

when you expand your territory, divide up and hold places of advantage.

Calculate the situation, and then move.

Those who know the principles of the circuitous and direct will be victorious.

This is armed struggle.[11]

The Book of Military Administration says:

It is because words cannot be clearly heard in battle, drums and gongs are used;

it is because troops cannot see each other clearly in battle, flags and pennants are used.[12]

(continued on page 93)

13 There is a time and a place for different kinds of communication, if you use them skillfully and appropriately. Sometimes, a gentle word of encouragement to a colleague will motivate him or her to complete a task; at other times, firm words of rebuke, even controlled anger, may be in order. In every case, though, the communication will be most effective if it comes from a selfless regard focused on achieving a future result, not punishing a perceived wrong in the past.

14 Sun Tzu understands the power of sheer spectacle, and advocates the use of many torches, drums, flags, and pennants for effect. The rumble of drums and the sea of flickering torches and dancing flags and pennants inspire a general's men and place fear in his enemy. By involving both the eyes and the ears of his soldiers, a general ensures they pay attention, act in unison, and execute his strategy as planned.

When a group is united with a clear strategy to achieve a common goal, the power of the group itself has a moderating, yet empowering, effect on the individuals. The energy of those who would charge forth recklessly is harnessed and channeled into more productive actions, and those who would be reluctant to act at all discover the courage to join the battle and contribute to the effort.

Therefore, in night battles use torches and drums;

in day battles use flags and pennants.[13]

Drums, gongs, flags, and pennants are used to unite men's eyes and ears.

When the men are united, the brave cannot advance alone, the cowardly cannot retreat alone.

These are the principles for employing a large number of troops.

Therefore, in night battles, use many torches and drums, and in day battles, use many flags and pennants in order to influence men's eyes and ears.[14]

(continued on page 95)

15 At the beginning of any conflict, tensions and energy run high, and unskilled adversaries filled with negative energy want to take immediate action. Sun Tzu's advice is to avoid such opponents through formlessness. Instead of wearing them down by attacking them or defending against them, wear them down through the passage of time. As you conserve your energy, they exhaust theirs. Then, when their energy level is at its lowest, you can move with advantage.

Though your adversaries' negative energy probably doesn't run its course over years, the philosophy of civil rights activist Martin Luther King Jr., honored for his message of peaceful conflict resolution, exemplifies the virtues of patience and selflessness that avoid the temptation to strike back. In a sermon delivered at Dexter Avenue Baptist Church, in Montgomery, Alabama, on November 17, 1957, he said:

> You just keep loving people and keep loving them, even though they're mistreating you. Here's the person who is a neighbor, and this person is doing something wrong to you and all of that. Just keep being friendly to that person. Keep loving them. Don't do anything to embarrass them. Just keep loving them, and they can't stand it too long. Oh, they react in many ways in the beginning. They react with bitterness because they're mad because you love them like that. They react with guilt feelings, and sometimes they'll hate you a little more at that transition period, but just keep loving them. And by the power of your love they will break down under the load. That's love, you see. It is redemptive, and this is why Jesus says love. There's something about love that builds up and is creative. There is something about hate that tears down and is destructive. So love your enemies.

The energy of the army can be dampened, and the general's mind can be dampened.

Therefore, in the morning, energy is high, but during the day energy begins to flag;

and in the evening, energy is exhausted.

Therefore, those skilled in the use of force avoid high energy, and strike when energy is exhausted.

This is the way to manage energy.[15]

(continued on page 97)

16 This approach is also a form of the active inaction described in chapter 3, where you wear your adversaries down and unravel them. In time their anger will dissipate and they will feel disorderly, clamorous, fatigued, or hungry. By giving your adversaries reasons not to fight, and by not perpetuating their hatred, you make them lose interest in prolonging the conflict. In other words, you provide them ample logical excuses to give up their mission.

17 Inevitably, you will face tough adversaries who possess extraordinary intelligence and organization. They secure favorable positions while they negate your strengths. They too become formless and may even have you chase after a minor advantage in the hopes of exposing your strengths and weaknesses. According to Sun Tzu, when you find yourself outsmarted or outmaneuvered, you should adapt to the situation. Don't stubbornly push forward a strategy no longer relevant to the new challenge. Instead, exercise caution and prudence until you can ascertain your adversaries' strengths and weaknesses.

18 Sun Tzu again shows his compassion by advocating that the general spare a defeated enemy.

Some scholars have argued that Sun Tzu's primary aim here is a practical one, because trying to ruthlessly eliminate a desperate opponent could give the enemy troops renewed vigor for fighting and result in still more bloodshed and destruction.

Indeed, practicality was evident in Sun Tzu's decisions but it was always coupled with compassion. His overall desire was to stop aggression, not to prolong it. You too can exhibit this compassion toward those who display none toward you. Hating your adversaries accomplishes nothing, but kindness opens up opportunities for healing and reconciliation. The more power you possess, the more important compassion becomes, to offset the potential harm you can cause by wielding your power carelessly or vindictively.

Disciplined, wait for disorder;

calm, wait for clamor.

This is the way to manage the mind.

Near, wait for the distant;

rested, wait for the fatigued;

full, wait for the hungry.

This is the way to manage strength.[16]

Do not do battle with well-ordered flags;

do not do battle with well-regulated formations.

This is the way to manage adaptation.

Therefore, the principles of warfare are:

Do not attack an enemy that has the high ground;

do not attack an enemy that has his back to a hill;

do not pursue feigned retreats;

do not attack elite troops;

do not swallow the enemy's bait;[17]

do not thwart an enemy retreating home.

If you surround the enemy, leave an outlet;

do not press an enemy that is cornered.

These are the principles of warfare.[18]

◆ Although a few scholars believe the number nine in this chapter's title is literal, I agree with the majority of scholars, who conclude that the number nine here is symbolic of a limitless amount, such as "Ninth Heaven" (the highest point in heaven, according to Chinese mythology). The nine changes, therefore, indicate the limitless changes or possibilities that the present and future hold. Yet within this seeming chaos, certain patterns emerge. Sun Tzu identifies these recurring patterns within the five types of Ground (environment) and counsels certain strategies to effectively work with each type. The variations that accompany these patterns, however, give rise to endlessly unique permutations—the nine changes—which require flexibility to manage.

According to Sun Tzu, the best way to approach the many changes in your life is to continually adapt to your ever-evolving world. Stubbornly forcing worn-out strategies in new situations or clinging to outmoded ideologies leads to defeat, or worse. Instead, prepare yourself as much as possible for the patterns and contingencies and avoid dangerous excesses, such as recklessness or cowardice, that may limit your ability to remain flexible in the face of the situation as it actually arises.

1 Like chapter 7, this chapter opens with the general receiving his powers from the emperor, who in turn receives his from the population. No one acts alone, and no one succeeds or fails alone. When other people support your efforts and depend on your success, you have additional resources and motivation to overcome your problems and resolve your conflicts.

8 □ Nine Changes

Sun Tzu said:

Generally, the principles of warfare are:

The general receives his commands from the ruler, assembles the armies, and mobilizes the masses.[1]

(continued on page 101)

2 In chapter 10, "Ground Formation," and chapter 11, "Nine Grounds," Sun Tzu more thoroughly defines difficult ground and the other types of ground mentioned in this set of verses. This preview, however, is a helpful introduction. Though the types of ground listed here refer specifically to landscapes or environments that an army might encounter in military campaigns, you will encounter situations in your everyday life that have similar characteristics.

Difficult ground is where the army has trouble passing through, such as swamps and wetlands. A prudent general eschews remaining on ground that hinders his movement because such ground limits his options. Likewise, you shouldn't stay in an environment that limits your options; if trouble arrives, you want all avenues to be open to you so you can respond freely and effectively.

3 On intersecting ground, the army is surrounded by enemies, allies, and potential allies. Because of the tenuous relationships that exist in such a diverse and dynamic environment, you should strengthen your relationships with your allies and forge new relationships with potential allies to keep your adversary from attracting them and diverting them to his or her corner.

4 Open ground is where the army can come and go freely. Although this seems to be the ideal environment and opposite of difficult ground, open ground has its own dangers. It increases your options, but also increases the options for your adversaries, who may gain the advantage and attack you.

5 Surrounded ground is the ultimate trap for the army. The entrance is small and narrow, allowing only a few in, and the exit is circuitous. Your adversary may have more knowledge, resources, and support than you. So when you must enter this environment, enter it with ample strength in preparation for the worst.

Do not camp on difficult ground.[2]

Unite with your allies on intersecting ground.[3]

Do not stay on open ground.[4]

Be prepared on surrounded ground.[5]

(continued on page 103)

6 On deadly ground, the army hits a dead end and has nowhere to go but through enemy forces. Sun Tzu advises you to fight on deadly ground because, with all your options cut off, you must muster all your effort just to survive the predicament.

7 Taken literally, this verse seems to say that there are routes, armies, walled cities, and grounds that will bring you calamity if you choose to take them. However, within the context of the selflessness and compassion found throughout The Art of War, and especially in light of the very next verse, this verse is more accurately interpreted to mean that there are logical *and* moral considerations to take into account while trying to gain an advantage. In other words, just because you *can* do something does not mean you *should* do it. When you think about the welfare of others instead of just yourself, you will find that there are indeed actions you shouldn't take and situations you shouldn't enter into. Such moderation of the ego and its motivations requires tremendous wisdom and self-control—and a willingness to endure harsh criticism.

Therefore, before engaging in a conflict, determine the ethical line you will not cross. This line could be based on your principles or beliefs, but whatever it is, you can be proud knowing you don't need to descend to immorality to achieve what you want in life.

8 Sun Tzu departs from ancient China's culture, where respect and obeisance toward elders and superiors were paramount, illustrating his ethical and intellectual transcendence of both time and place. Seemingly unconcerned for his own welfare—whether he'll be rewarded or punished—Sun Tzu places more value on making the right and natural (in accord with the Way) decision than on blindly following the orders of an authority figure.

Do battle on deadly ground.[6]

There are routes not to be taken;

there are armies not to be attacked;

there are walled cities not to be besieged;

there are grounds not to be penetrated;[7]

there are commands not to be obeyed.[8]

(continued on page 105)

9 The "five advantages" are not the five grounds discussed at the beginning of this chapter but the five main factors of warfare found in chapter 1: Way (unity in moral purpose with others), Heaven (atmosphere and moods), Ground (landscape), General (beneficial traits of a leader), and Law (organization and management of resources). Just as he advised in the previous verse against blindly following orders, Sun Tzu here questions the wisdom of always following established rules—even important rules.

After all, what good is having advantages in the five factors of Way, Heaven, Ground, General, and Law if your situation changes overnight? What were advantages could now be disadvantages. In addition, even careful analysis of the five most important factors cannot encompass all the countless possibilities—the nine changes—you will face in the future. Sun Tzu even breaks away from the ancient symbolism of the number five here, much like how the ancient teaching of the five elements (earth, metal, wood, fire, water—see chapter 5, annotation 5) seems rudimentary next to the modern periodic table of the chemical elements. This verse is Sun Tzu's unequivocal way of emphasizing the importance of adapting to our ever-changing world based on new information and what's currently happening, not on outdated, irrelevant knowledge and traditions.

10 To complement your analysis of the advantages and disadvantages on the five main factors in chapter 1, you can also carefully consider the advantages and anticipate the disadvantages in the myriad possible new factors and situations you may encounter. With flexibility, you quickly adapt to changes to take advantage of new opportunities (fulfill your calculations) and prevent new problems (remove your difficulties). Although you cannot cover all the infinite changes, you plan for what is most probable, which is much better than leaving your situation to chance.

Therefore, the general who knows the advantages of the nine changes knows how to use the troops.

If the general does not know the advantages of the nine changes, even if he knows the lay of the land, he will not be able to take advantage of the ground.

He who commands an army but does not know the principles of the nine changes, even if he is familiar with the five advantages, will not be able to best use his troops.[9]

Therefore, the intelligent general contemplates both the advantages and disadvantages.

Contemplating the advantages, he fulfills his calculations; contemplating the disadvantages, he removes his difficulties.[10]

(*continued on page 107*)

11 One way to avoid disasters is to block your adversaries from proceeding with their plans and doing you harm. Show them the potential negative consequences they face if they continue. Make their paths circuitous and slow them down by distracting them. Show them better gains (baited or real) if they move in a different direction. Your objective is to pacify your adversaries and make them harmless, not to destroy them.

12 In speeches made to the U.S. Congress on March 29, 2007, and May 9, 2007, Robert Gates, the twenty-second U.S. secretary of defense and former president of Texas A&M University, cited this verse by Sun Tzu that explains why effective peacekeeping takes preparation, not passivity. He then added, "This holds true for our national defense today." George Washington, the first president of the United States, shared the same belief when he said in his first State of the Union address on January 8, 1790: "To be prepared for war is one of the most effectual means of preserving peace."

Therefore, subjugate the neighboring rulers with potential disadvantages, labor the neighboring rulers with constant matters, and have the neighboring rulers rush after advantages.[11]

So the principles of warfare are:

Do not depend on the enemy not coming, but depend on our readiness against him.

Do not depend on the enemy not attacking, but depend on our position that cannot be attacked. [12]

(continued on page 109)

13 While the first three dangerous traits are straightforward, the final two might be perplexing. Given the context of this section, however, being moral or fond of the people means having these traits in excess and without regard to the unique circumstances, such as being self-righteous or doting.

For example, because of his rigid moral beliefs, the general might refuse to engage in necessary deception and thus could put his soldiers needlessly in harm's way. In everyday life, you might value honesty to the point of callously calling attention to someone's faults or disclosing the whereabouts of a political dissident. Such behavior shows naivete more than integrity. Likewise, you might unwisely indulge every whim of your children and thereby encourage their negative behavior, instead of showing them real love, which involves boundaries and discipline. Henry David Thoreau, a popular American naturalist and transcendentalist, conveyed the irrationality behind these behaviors when he wrote, "Circumstances are not rigid and unyielding, but our habits are rigid." Thus, any positive trait can become dangerous if exhibited in excess and in a manner inappropriate to the situation.

14 Historical accounts abound of military generals bringing misfortune to their armies and their nations due to their recklessness, cowardice, temper, naivete, or laxity. Admitting to your flaws might be disheartening, but only if you cherish your ego more than the well-being of others. When you become selfless and think about other people, you can matter-of-factly identify your deficiencies and quickly improve upon them. Sun Tzu believes that only then can you avert the many possible tragedies lurking in the problems and conflicts you encounter in life.

Therefore, there are five dangerous traits of a general:

He who is reckless can be killed.

He who is cowardly can be captured.

He who is quick tempered can be insulted.

He who is moral can be shamed.

He who is fond of the people can be worried.[13]

These five traits are faults in a general, and are disastrous in warfare.

The army's destruction, and the death of the general are due to these five dangerous traits.

They must be examined.[14]

◆ Army maneuvers are the strategic movements the army undertakes when confronted with difficult terrain and crafty enemies. Once you have adjusted to the difficulties of the terrain and assessed the wide variety of possibilities it offers you (see chapter 8), you can then *act* to take advantage of its beneficial features. In this chapter, Sun Tzu also counsels you to look behind an adversary's surface appearance to understand, and respond effectively to, his or her true motivations.

1 A mountain presents a substantial obstacle to an army. Rather than struggling needlessly over mountain passes, the army can overcome them effortlessly and efficiently by sticking to the low ground—much as water simply flows around a rock. To Sun Tzu, struggling doesn't necessarily equate to making progress. Likewise, attacking a difficult problem head-on might result in a flurry of activity, but a more efficient and enlightened approach might be to work around the problem, patiently searching for an opening that will allow you to easily pass through, as an army might circumvent a mountain by passing through a valley.

2 Holding high ground gives the army a clear view of the enemy below, and the slope slows an attacking enemy, preventing an ambush. Facing the sunny side—having the sun at the army's back so that the sun illuminates the hill sloping down away in front—allows the army to see what is ahead of it and move with safety.

Wherever you are, position yourself so you can easily see your adversary's whereabouts and be able to prepare early if she decides to attack you. Conversely, don't confront your adversary if she is in a position to plainly see your approach and to prepare her defenses early.

9 □ Army Maneuvers

Sun Tzu said:

Generally, on positioning the army and observing the enemy:

To cross mountains, stay close to the valleys;[1]

observe on high ground and face the sunny side.

If the enemy holds the high ground, do not ascend and do battle with him.

This is positioning the army in the mountains.[2]

(continued on page 113)

3 | A river divides an army and its strength. Thus, Sun Tzu's strategy calls for attacking an enemy when it is in a vulnerable position, and for taking care to avoid confrontation when you yourself are divided and weakened. During such times, seek safety, such as can be found in the support of family and friends. You are not alone in your ordeal. Similar to the sun shining down a dark path, family and friends can help you see what's ahead and where best to go.

4 | Swamps and wetlands mire the army. However, positioning soldiers near grass provides them more solid ground for easier movement. Trees to the back serve to protect soldiers from an enemy attack as they struggle to pass through this difficult terrain.

Note how Sun Tzu transforms a terrain that hinders into a terrain that's tolerable, and converts a potentially dangerous terrain into one that provides protection. With a similar confident outlook, you too can find something positive in a negative situation.

For example, if you are consistently failing to find resolution in a particular conflict, don't give up and wallow in your misery, as an army might become bogged down in a swamp or wetland. Instead, view the time of trouble as an opportunity to uncover the deepest roots of your problem—which perhaps arise from unexamined core beliefs or ingrained habits that consistently hinder you. Gaining such personal insight can help you both to finally resolve your immediate situation and also to more quickly recognize similar situations when they arise again—and hence give you the ability to proactively address the situation before it blossoms into another full-blown conflict.

5 | In ancient China, a soldier carried his shield on his left arm; hence, the army's right side was most vulnerable and needed to be backed by high ground. As the army focused on its front, it needed to ensure its back was safe from enemy attacks.

When faced with a conflict, focus on the challenges in front of you. Worrying about your right side or your back only divides your attention and, in turn, hinders your progress. If you are overwhelmed from facing too many problems at once, choose to focus on just one, or you risk accomplishing nothing at all.

After crossing a river, you must stay far away from it.

If the enemy crosses a river, do not meet him in the water.

When half of his forces has crossed, it will then be advantageous to strike.

If you want to do battle with the enemy, do not position your forces near the water facing the enemy;

take high ground facing the sunny side, and do not position downstream.

This is positioning the army near rivers.[3]

After crossing swamps and wetlands, strive to quickly get through them, and do not linger.

If you do battle in swamps and wetlands, you must position close to grass, with the trees to your back.

This is positioning the army in swamps and wetlands.[4]

On level ground, position on places that are easy to maneuver with your right backed by high ground, with the dangerous ground in front, and safe ground to the back.

This is positioning the army on level ground.[5]

(continued on page 115)

6 | In spite of the difficulties of mountains, rivers, swamps and wetlands, and level ground, the four corresponding positions show how the army can survive in less than ideal conditions. Thus, whether your conflict is difficult or easy, focus on occupying an advantageous position, with your safety as the primary concern.

According to Chinese legend, the Yellow Emperor, or Huang Di, ruled from 2697 to 2597 BCE, and was the inventor of the martial arts. He ruled All-Under-Heaven after he defeated the Red Emperor to the south, the Green Emperor to the east, the White Emperor to the west, and the Black Emperor to the north. To conquer his opponents in all four areas, he and his army traversed through all the types of terrain Sun Tzu has discussed, yet moved with relative ease and safety because he sought advantages even in tough environments.

7 | Obtaining safety and an advantage through these four positions will lead to certain victory. That victory may not come right away, but with time, the right openings will eventually present themselves to the army and allow them to gain the advantage. The only question is whether the army will survive long enough to take advantage of the opportunity. Similarly, your own situation may not seem promising today, but if you continue to secure an advantageous position, tomorrow might reveal unexpected opportunities that allow you to resolve the most difficult of problems or conflicts.

8 | The general can find advantage even in mundane terrains such as hills and embankments—using them to provide the army elevation and protection, in this example. In your everyday life, observe your normal surroundings from a different angle or in different light. Sometimes you don't need a change of setting to make your life easier, you just need to make the most out of your current one.

These are the four positions advantageous to the army, which enabled the Yellow Emperor to conquer four rulers.[6]

Generally, the army prefers high ground and dislikes low ground, values the sunny side and despises the shady side, nourishes its health and occupies places with resources, and avoids numerous sicknesses.

These factors mean certain victory.[7]

Where there are hills and embankments, you must position on the sunny side, with the hills and embankments to your right back.

These are advantages to the army.

Use the ground for assistance.[8]

(continued on page 117)

9 The rain may have subsided, but the current it produced in the river could still be dangerous. Here Sun Tzu emphasizes the need to have patience for the right moment when progress can be made. If you face an enraged adversary, often the simplest way to resolve the conflict is to just give him time to regain control of his emotions. If you try to force your will too early, while he is still angry and irrational, you won't make any progress and risk making it worse.

10 Sun Tzu uses poetic language in this verse to describe entrapping types of terrain. Heaven's Wells are steeply inclined in all directions with water below; Heaven's Prisons are steeply inclined on three sides with one opening where it's easy to enter but difficult to leave; Heaven's Nets are thick forests and undergrowth; Heaven's Pits consist of muddy soil where chariots cannot pass; and Heaven's Fissures are long, narrow paths between mountains.

All of these terrains limit the army's movement, and soldiers making their way through them risk getting entangled. Similar to an entangled army, you may have great strength, but if your situation ties you down or severely slows you, what good is your great strength? For instance, you may have great wealth, but if all that money heightens your suspicion of other people, causes you to rest on your laurels, and spoils your children—all of which foster much unhappiness—what good is it? Avoid such common pitfalls. In case of a personal crisis, make sure your resources enable you to settle it, not make it worse.

When the rainwater rises and descends down to where you want to cross, wait until it settles.[9]

Where there is ground with impassable ravines, Heaven's Wells, Heaven's Prisons, Heaven's Nets, Heaven's Pits, and Heaven's Fissures, you must march quickly away from them.

Do not approach them.

When we distance from them, draw the enemy to approach them.

When we move to face the enemy, he will have them at his back.[10]

(*continued on page 119*)

11 With this verse, Sun Tzu shifts his focus from finding the advantage in various terrains, to carefully observing the enemy in order to glean important information about him or her. He points out that difficult terrain is doubly treacherous: it can hinder the army's movements and conceal spies and ambushes.

12 In times of conflict, military generals not only observe the opponent's actions, but also ascertain the intentions behind those actions. By knowing the enemy's motivations, the general can determine how best to respond in spite of the outward displays of enemy hostility or sycophantism. Similarly, if you pay close attention to the real meaning behind the words and actions of your adversaries, you can conclude whether those words or actions should be taken seriously and decide on your best response.

When the army is flanked by high ground, wetlands, tall reeds and grass, mountain forests, or areas with thick undergrowth, you must search carefully and thoroughly, because these are places where men lie in ambush or where spies hide.[11]

If the enemy is close and remains quiet, he occupies a natural stronghold.

If the enemy is far away and challenges you to do battle, he wants you to advance, because he occupies level ground that is to his advantage.[12]

(continued on page 121)

13 As the general stands on a hilltop surveying what the enemy is pretending to do, feigning and flanking, he also watches what doesn't lie: the natural world—the dust and the animals. He sees beneath the surface, down to the bare truth.

To determine your adversary's intentions, observe the surrounding environment. Although adversaries may deceive you and hide their true actions behind false movements, the environments and conditions they operate under do not. For instance, observe the people close to your opponents—their family, friends, allies, and even enemies. How do they behave, and what can you discern from their behavior?

14 If your adversary's words are inconsistent with his actions, Sun Tzu advises you to believe the actions, because words can more easily mask nefarious intentions. This idea is nothing new; as the psalmist poetically observed, words can be a particularly treacherous method of deceit:

> My companion laid hands on a friend
> and violated a covenant with me
> with speech smoother than butter,
> but with a heart set on war;
> with words that were softer than oil,
> but in fact were drawn swords.
> *(Psalm 55:20–21)*

The old saying is true: actions do speak louder than words.

15 Anger often motivates people to take aggressive action, but excessive aggression may indicate a loss of control or an attempt to compensate for weakness. Your adversary may simply want to test your reaction and could retreat at the first sign of your show of strength.

If trees move, he is advancing;

if there are obstacles placed in the undergrowth, he wants to make us suspicious;

if the birds take flight, he is lying in ambush;

if the animals are in fear, he is preparing to attack;

if dust is high in straight columns, his chariots are advancing;

if dust is low and wide, his infantry is advancing.

If the dust is scattered, he is gathering wood;

if the dust is sparse, coming and going, he is encamping.[13]

If he speaks humbly, but increases warfare readiness, he will advance.[14]

If he speaks belligerently and advances aggressively, he will retreat.[15]

(continued on page 123)

16 Here, Sun Tzu means that when an adversary speaks with uncharacteristic humility or offers apologies for every trifling offense, he wants to secure your favor.

17 If your adversary commits by taking preparatory steps, he will likely follow through with the commitment. It is better to prepare for aggression than to hope that it will not materialize. As mentioned in chapter 8, "Do not depend on the enemy not coming, but depend on our readiness against him." This verse contrasts the calm, measured preparation for battle against the bluff and bluster of aggression, implying that a calm and rational mind is far more dangerous than an angry, red-in-the-face adversary.

18 Sun Tzu advises against doing anything rash when you see erratic behavior from your adversary. Instead, pause and observe carefully to discover if his apparent irrationality has purpose, or if it is a genuine vulnerability that you can use to your advantage. As always, a calm, rational, self-possessed mind motivated by understanding and compassion is your greatest ally in the heat of conflict.

19 Subtle clues from your adversary's body language often reveal real intentions or level of strength. You can confirm your perception and expose his strengths and weaknesses by examining his conduct in times of great stress or struggle.

20 Military officers are usually chosen for their strong leadership qualities. If even they are frustrated, there must be extreme hardship within the army. Thus, if you see those who are normally stoic lose their temper, they are likely tired or experiencing great trouble.

If he speaks apologetically, he needs a rest.[16]

If his light chariots move first and take position on the flanks, he is setting up for battle.

If he seeks peace without a treaty, he is calculating.

If he sets up his troops rapidly, he is expecting reinforcements.[17]

If half his troops advance and half his troops retreat, he is trying to lure you.[18]

If the troops lean on their weapons, they are hungry.

If the troops who draw water drink first, they are thirsty.

If he sees advantage but does not take it, he is tired.[19]

If birds gather, he is not there.

If his troops cry at night, they are afraid.

If the army is unsettled, the general is weak.

If the enemy's flags and pennants move about, he is in chaos.

If the officers are irritable, they are exhausted.[20]

(continued on page 125)

21 If the army uses all of its remaining resources, paying no attention to conservation or housekeeping, it is in desperate straits. Based on the context of this section, this last-ditch effort comes from a position of weakness, not strength. Look for similar desperate behavior from your adversary; do not cause her ruin, but with your overwhelming advantage, show her the futility of the conflict and convince her to give up.

22 Touching on the five dangerous traits of a general from chapter 8, Sun Tzu gives examples of negative consequences arising from poor leadership. To him, behavior guided by impulse rather than by principle or strategy highlights shortcomings. Even doing good deeds such as rewarding people loses its effect if done excessively. Punishment may be necessary to correct people, but it demoralizes them if doled out too frequently. If your adversaries display any similar traits, they will divide their allies instead of uniting them. This is your clue that they have shaky support and will crumble at the first sign of trouble. You can also seek potential allies from among those who are turned off by your adversaries' behavior and further increase your own strength.

23 Your opponent will display anger but if his threats are not immediately followed by corresponding aggressive action, then he is not rash or out of control, but instead weak, slow, or trying to lure you into a trap. No matter how strong you are, you will be thwarted if you are lured into an emotional reaction or to an unfavorable situation where your options are limited. Thus, investigate the reason behind the incongruence of his anger and lack of action. Sun Tzu advises you to exercise caution and prudence by putting safety before retaliation, convenience, or easy opportunity.

If his horses are fed grain and his men meat; if he no longer hangs up cooking pots, and does not return to camp, he is desperate.[21]

If troops constantly gather in small groups and whisper together, he has lost his men.

If he gives out rewards frequently, he is running out of resources.

If he gives out punishments frequently, he is in dire straits.

If he is brutal at first, and then fears the masses, he is the extreme of ineptitude.[22]

If he comes with offerings, he wants to rest.

If his troops confront you with anger, but do not do battle or leave their position, he must be investigated.[23]

(continued on page 127)

24 In war as in any conflict, Sun Tzu reminds us that there are no guarantees. What you think is an easy opportunity could very well be a trap set by cunning adversaries. It is important to exercise caution and prudence even in situations where you seemingly have tremendous advantage over your adversaries. Although you will likely want to quickly and fully seize an opportunity that presents itself, you should do so only after deliberation—and if you will not give up your position of invincibility. Even if you miss this opportunity, others will come in the future. But if you risk your position of invincibility, you won't be around to take any opportunities at all. As mathematics professor and investment trader Nassim Nicholas Taleb astutely observed: "It does not matter how frequently something succeeds if failure is too costly to bear." Sometimes potential gains simply don't justify the potential heavy costs.

25 Sun Tzu assures you that you don't need extraordinary skills to protect yourself from your opponents. You can achieve sufficient ability to resolve all your conflicts and problems if you leverage your strength, observe your adversary, and gain the support of the people around you. Going to extremes or doing things in excess will not only impede your progress but will make matters worse. For example, even if you dislike your adversary intensely, you don't need to mount personal attacks on him or her to gain the support of potential allies. In fact, such attacks might turn off those allies completely. Instead, explain the logical reasons why they should join in your effort.

26 Sun Tzu believes in planning as if the enemy will attack and has the ability to do so. Although this seems like an alarmist or overly anxious perspective, by addressing your potential vulnerabilities, you gain peace of mind knowing you prepared yourself for all plausible problems. When you have a plan for the worst-case scenario, anything else that transpires will seem effortless.

In warfare, numbers may not necessarily be an advantage;

do not advance aggressively.[24]

It is enough to consolidate your strength, calculate the enemy, and get support from your men.[25]

One who lacks strategic planning and underestimates the enemy will be captured.[26]

(continued on page 129)

27 Trust and discipline go hand in hand. Without trust, discipline becomes ineffective. Without discipline, the army becomes ineffective. An important attribute that leads to both trust and discipline is benevolence. If your supporters believe you care about them, you can discipline them, and they, in turn, will unite in purpose. They will believe you care about them when you try to help them after they ask for help. They will then follow even blunt orders. They will trust what you say and follow your instruction immediately without hesitation or lingering doubts. But if you try to help them when they don't ask, then you might appear bossy even if you make courteous suggestions. Thus, make sure your benevolence is actually beneficial, and not merely perceived so in your mind.

The difference between the deception employed by the enemy discussed in this chapter and the deception employed by Sun Tzu in chapter 1 is benevolence. The enemy's deception is undertaken to gain an edge to destroy his or her opposition. Sun Tzu's deception also seeks to achieve an advantage, but with the purpose of *preventing* destruction. He gains advantage not to ruin his enemy but to render the enemy harmless and stop the suffering of all involved.

28 According to Sun Tzu, consistency helps build trust. Consistency also connotes a sense of fairness shown to everyone. Implied in the verse is that the general also lives by the same rules, because the soldiers are "in accord with the general." When each person receives equal treatment, there is nothing dividing him or her from the others, and everyone, from top to bottom, unites in a single purpose.

If one punishes the troops before their loyalty is formed, they will be disobedient.

If they are disobedient, they will be difficult to use.

If one does not punish the troops after their loyalty is formed, they cannot be used.

Therefore, if he commands them by benevolence, and unifies them by discipline, this is called certain victory.[27]

If commands are consistently enforced when training men, they will be obedient;

if commands are not consistently enforced when training men, they will be disobedient.

If commands are consistently executed, they are in accord with the general.[28]

◆ In this chapter, Sun Tzu explains six grounds, or types of environment in which you might find yourself when confronted with conflict. He explores their dangers, but also highlights the advantages they offer you against your adversary. These six grounds are the first set of a total of sixteen grounds that Sun Tzu discusses in The Art of War. This chapter also explores the six paths of defeat, which he urges you to avoid because they can cause unnecessary hardship and suffering for you and those around you. To successfully negotiate these variables you must embrace the paradox of selflessness: the more you forget about yourself and shun glory, the more people will remember you and glorify you.

1 Sun Tzu lists six types of ground—the literal landscape where soldiers march and camp—which, as we learned in chapter 1, is one of the five crucial factors that determine the outcome in warfare. In chapter 11, "Nine Grounds," he lists ten more types of ground, for a total of sixteen. These aren't meant to be a comprehensive list, but rather a set of possibilities, the combinations of which can be limitless (similar to the concept of infinite possibilities discussed in chapter 8).

Understanding the intricacies of each type of ground can help you see the intrinsic advantages that each offers. This, in turn, will give you the advantage, even in the most troubling ground, over your adversary. That is not to say you can ignore each ground's risks and dangers; you should recognize them to avoid disaster. However, if you want to do more than just avoid disaster, and instead make progress and solve your problems, you can dig deeper and discover benefits in your environment.

10 □ Ground Formation

Sun Tzu said:

The grounds are accessible, entrapping, stalemated, narrow, steep, and expansive.[1]

(continued on page 133)

2 When your unique abilities or attributes allow you to enter a ground that your adversary cannot, it is called accessible ground. In accessible ground, the army can secure a sustainable advantage on the sunny side of high ground. This represents a place that enables you to observe your adversary in safety and at full strength before you take decisive action.

Convenient supply routes connote a way to recharge your energy where your focus, strength, and purpose never fade. For you, this might mean eating right, exercising, meditating, and the like. With all your fundamental needs abundantly met, you are able to remain calm and alert—instead of becoming desperate or exhausted—in stressful situations.

3 Entering entrapping ground requires careful consideration and, if the army chooses to engage in battle, a commitment to see the battle through, because it cannot easily retreat. If you think you can handle your adversary and work with him or her, then go forward. But if you stubbornly choose to take on a difficult adversary in this environment and you run into trouble, remember—the blame is your own! In such cases, accepting responsibility for your own decisions and mistakes, rather than trying to find a scapegoat, will allow you to more swiftly correct the problem you created.

4 Quite the opposite from entering accessible ground, entering stalemated ground gives the army a disadvantage instead of an advantage. Stalemated ground is where you and your adversary have both made some progress, but to go farther would be risky, much like two armies converging on opposite sides of a river—neither can cross without dividing and becoming vulnerable.

If you find yourself in this kind of deadlocked situation, you might mistakenly try to break the impasse by letting down your guard and showing kindness to your enemy. Unfortunately, your adversary might fail to reciprocate your goodwill gesture and instead take advantage of the vulnerability you exposed by making such a gesture. A better way to break the impasse is to maintain your core position of invincibility and limit your risk by testing how your adversary reacts to a *small* gesture of kindness. If he reciprocates, proceed a little more; if not, you haven't lost much.

If you can go through but the enemy cannot, it is called accessible.

For accessible ground, first take the high and the sunny side, and convenient supply routes.

You then do battle with the advantage.[2]

If you can go through but it is difficult to go back, it is called entrapping.

For entrapping ground, if the enemy is unprepared, advance and defeat him.

If the enemy is prepared, and you advance and are not victorious, it will be difficult to go back;

this is disadvantageous.[3]

If it is not advantageous to advance or for the enemy to advance, it is called stalemated.

For stalemated ground, though the enemy offers you advantage, do not advance.

Withdraw.

If you strike them when half has advanced, this is advantageous.[4]

(continued on page 135)

5 If an army is weak, it should seek to occupy narrow ground because such terrain will divide the enemy and make him weaker at the point of battle. Likewise, you should secure narrow ground in situations where you don't want to bear the brunt of your adversaries, but instead want to make steady progress with them over time.

In narrow ground occupied by the enemy, the army cannot enter all at once and so the few who enter first are vulnerable. In such a precarious scenario, you must determine if you have sufficient strength compared with your adversary. Entrapping ground and narrow ground are similar in constraint but different in the time and place of vulnerability: entrapping ground limits your exit, whereas narrow ground limits your entry.

6 Steep ground is the same as high ground, an advantageous environment where the army can easily see its enemy as he expends energy to reach the army from below, and the army confronts him at full energy from above. Likewise, you should take the moral, psychological, and intellectual high ground when facing your adversaries. You ensure your safety and increase your effectiveness because you don't waste your time and energy chasing after petty matters but address only important matters that truly affect you.

Conversely, if your adversary has high ground and an invincible position, accept the futility of trying to force progress where none can be made. As Sun Tzu stated in chapter 4, "Those skilled in warfare can make themselves invincible, but cannot necessarily cause the enemy to be vulnerable." Even if you're skillful, you can't always be successful, because there are sometimes factors outside your influence.

For narrow ground, we must occupy it first;

be prepared and wait for the enemy.

If the enemy occupies it first, and is prepared, do not follow him.

If he is not prepared, follow him.[5]

For steep ground, if you occupy it first, occupy the high on the sunny side and wait for the enemy.

If the enemy occupies it first, withdraw;

do not follow him.[6]

(continued on page 137)

7 Sun Tzu favors the army having superior strength, not merely equal strength. Equal strength prolongs the conflict because neither side has sufficient power to quickly stop the other. Because expansive ground is wide-open space, it is an environment with few limitations and numerous options for both sides. Neither you nor your opponent will have many weaknesses that can be exploited. Unless you have a lop-sided superiority over your adversary, she will find ways to elude your strategies in expansive ground.

In normal situations in life, equality usually means balance and harmony. But in the disharmonious situation of a conflict, balance can be a hindrance; *in*equality is what helps put a quick end to the disorder. This is analogous to a sick person relying on medicine to get well. The antibiotics must have overwhelming strength to quickly stop pathogens—if the medicine and pathogens were of equal strength, what good would taking the medicine be?

8 The six grounds themselves don't automatically give you advantage (or take advantage away from you). Rather, by closely and mindfully examining the ground you find yourself on, you can detect the advantage each type of ground has to offer, and gain the upper hand over your adversary, who might not study the ground as carefully. Sun Tzu urges you to take a serious, yet positive, perspective when approaching the six grounds, lest you be the one who does not reconnoiter the ground carefully, and find yourself faced with calamity.

9 Sun Tzu here turns from the six grounds to the six paths of defeat—six ominous situations you might encounter in a conflict. Unlike the grounds, these are not caused by your environment, but by your own doing. At times, you may want to blame bad luck, unfair people, or disadvantageous conditions for your dilemma. However, if you reflect back on both how you made your decision and how you acted, you will understand not only why you failed but also how you could have overcome your failure. Your past mistakes can help you to refine your actions and improve your chances of success in the future.

For expansive ground, if the forces are equal, it will be difficult to do battle.

Doing battle will not be advantageous.[7]

These are the six Ways of ground.

They are the general's responsibility, and must be examined.[8]

In warfare, there are flight, insubordination, deterioration, collapse, chaos, and setback.

These six situations are not caused by Heaven or Ground, but by the general.[9]

(continued on page 139)

10 If you have similar strength as your adversary, chances are you don't have much influence on her. If you then inexplicably send only one to confront her ten, how much greater are your chances of failing? You might not do something so foolish, but someone who is desperate, impatient, emotional, or careless might. This is analogous to attacking a walled city before making proper preparation, as described in chapter 3. It would be a suicide mission. Understandably, your supporters will flee (take "flight") from this senseless decision. They will retreat, and your predicament will have been caused by your own poor strategy, not by weakness or unfavorable position.

11 According to Sun Tzu, insubordination occurs when officers lack strictness and competence, and the rank-and-file soldiers thus show them little respect. When soldiers have no respect for their commanders, they will ignore orders that support the general's strategy. Although those around you may be strong, you, as their leader, should always serve as an example to them by being even stronger and disciplined beyond reproach. But you also need to forget your ego and status. Be the first to exert extra effort when needed, or to give up your comforts. This way, your supporters will have no doubts about your motivations, or complaints of unfairness, and they will unite when you call them to act. Jesus had this idea in mind when he washed his disciples' feet and then urged them "to wash one another's feet" (John 13:14).

12 Though you must always display your strength in order to keep your supporters in line, you cannot overcome all problems or conflicts by yourself, no matter how strong you are. You will run into tough situations where you will need other people's help. If they cannot help because they are unable, then you will have insufficient strength because you alone cannot do everything all the time. Over time, your energy and will continue to deteriorate.

If the forces are equal, and one attacks ten, this is called flight.[10]

If the troops are strong but the officers weak, this is called insubordination.[11]

If the officers are strong but the troops weak, this is called deterioration.[12]

(continued on page 141)

13 An insubordinate person means an undisciplined person, as evidenced by the lack of control over his or her emotion. Strong emotions, such as anger, cloud your thinking. The Art of War has shown how anger focuses your thoughts too much on yourself—your losses, your wants, your feelings—and prevents you from dwelling compassionately on the needs and well-being of others. If you allow anger to overwhelm you, you will fail to see the strength of your adversary (and your own weaknesses) and recklessly allow him or her to overwhelm you.

14 If the previous four ominous situations—flight, insubordination, deterioration, and collapse—converge, you will suffer chaos, the antithesis of hope and harmony. Indeed, this represents certain defeat.

15 Sun Tzu here comes full circle back to the first ominous situation, flight, where soldiers flee because the military general irresponsibly neglects to plan and employ his strategy according to the enemy's strength. If your adversary advances ten strong, don't respond with ten or fewer. If your adversary advances two, don't respond with two or fewer. To do so would cause your supporters to retreat, setting back your progress.

In a discussion about examining the cost and sacrifice of living a spiritual life, Jesus himself used a strikingly similar image: "Or what king, going out to wage war against another king, will not sit down first and consider whether he is able with ten thousand to oppose the one who comes against him with twenty thousand? If he cannot, then, while the other is still far away, he sends a delegation and asks for the terms of peace" (Luke 14:31–32). In both cases, rushing to action before completely understanding the cost of commitment leads to disappointment, setback, and defeat.

Note, however, that Sun Tzu believes size or numbers themselves don't matter; what matters is how you outmatch your opponent's strength at the time and place of convergence.

If the officers are angry and insubordinate, doing battle with the enemy under anger and insubordination, and the general does not know their abilities, this is called collapse.[13]

If the general is weak and not disciplined, his instructions not clear, the officers and troops lack discipline and their formation in disarray, this is called chaos.[14]

If the general cannot calculate his enemy, and uses a small number against a large number, his weak attacking the strong, and has no selected vanguard, this is called setback.[15]

(continued on page 143)

16 Sun Tzu again emphasizes the critical importance of studying these factors closely if you want to achieve victory. Although he outlines his lesson of the six paths of defeat from a different, more negative angle than the six grounds, you can nevertheless learn from bad situations. You learn what to do by looking at what *not* to do, which gives you freedom to come up with creative solutions to your problems.

17 Judging from this verse, the Way of the superior general doesn't seem all that superior. That is, you don't need extraordinary skills to understand your current environment, keep an eye on your adversary, and make the best of your circumstances to protect yourself from your adversary. Sun Tzu values leaders who can perform the basic, everyday tasks well over those who display flashy heroics in isolated incidents.

18 To control whether the general succeeds in all of his battles, he picks only the battles in which he can prevail. Otherwise, his men will suffer hardships and lose their lives, and the nation's citizens will be in similar peril. This is Sun Tzu's compassionate Way of warfare.

You will inevitably encounter conflicts you cannot win. For example, Sun Tzu's discussion of steep ground earlier in this chapter (see annotation 6) calls for withdrawal if your adversary secures an insurmountable advantage. In such adverse cases, consider yourself fortunate. Unlike most desperate and stubborn people who rush into impossible goals and cause themselves grief and suffering, you will know instead to stop and prepare further, build strength, and wait for the right time under the right conditions.

Making the right decision also requires that you have confidence in your ability and are able to courageously persuade superiors who may want to do things differently. As discussed in annotation 12 of chapter 3, this persuasion should not be considered insubordination, but true loyalty. Your only concern is the well-being of your superiors and your supporters, not reward or reprimand. This is the ultimate display of respect and trust.

These are the six Ways of defeat.

They are the general's responsibility, and must be examined.[16]

Formations of the ground assist the army.

To calculate the enemy, create conditions leading to victory, calculating the dangers and distances.

They are the Ways of the superior general.[17]

Those who do battle and know these are certain for victory.

Those who do battle and do not know these are certain for defeat.

Therefore, if the Way of warfare indicates certain victory, though the ruler does not want to do battle, the general may do battle.

If the Way of warfare indicates defeat, though the ruler wants to do battle, the general may not do battle.[18]

(continued on page 145)

19 Lao Tzu, author of the Tao Te Ching, said, "The military is a tool of misfortune, not the tool of honorable gentlemen. When using it out of necessity, calm detachment should be above all. Victorious but without glory." When you seek to gain glory or avoid punishment, your main concern lies with yourself and your own well-being, and you do not dispatch your resources effectively with the detachment that Lao Tzu described. You are guided by ulterior motives, not honorable ones. Sun Tzu echoes the same thought in this verse by stating that the general whose sole focus is on the problem at hand, and who shuns glory and status, will prevail and become beloved for generations to come.

When you forget glory, people want to glorify you because you glorify them with your selfless actions. When you forget your self-importance to protect them, they want to protect you because you're important to them. Jesus reflected this idea well when he said, "The greatest among you will be your servant. All who exalt themselves will be humbled, and all who humble themselves will be exalted" (Matthew 23:11–12). Selflessness that protects the multitude will be impossible for the world to forget.

20 In this verse, Sun Tzu may appear to promote treating soldiers like children. He did not; he treated them like able, responsible adults, but sincerely cared for them as if they were his own children. This distinction seems minor, but it is important. How would you care for your own children? You would go out of your way to protect them and look out for their best interests, neither cheating them nor causing them harm. At the same time, you wouldn't want them to shirk responsibility or become vulnerable to others, so you would teach and discipline them.

If you use this same approach with your supporters, they won't have any doubts about your love for them. Your bond with them will be tight, and they will go with you to the ends of the earth. You and they will be united in purpose, and will have achieved the Way, one of the five major factors that determine the outcome of conflicts, discussed in chapter 1.

Therefore, the general who does not advance to seek glory, or does not withdraw to avoid punishment, but cares for only the people's security and promotes the people's interests, is the nation's treasure.[19]

He looks upon his troops as children, and they will advance to the deepest valleys.

He looks upon his troops as his own children, and they will die with him.

If the general is kind to the troops, but cannot use them, or if the general loves the troops, but cannot command them, or if the general does not discipline the troops, but cannot establish order, the troops are like spoiled children and are useless.[20]

(continued on page 147)

21 Sun Tzu believes in securing superiority in all the variables of victory, including ground. To him, anything less is insufficient, a half effort.

You, too, should never settle for half measures. Knowing only yourself and your adversary might give you a false sense of security that you'll succeed. Sun Tzu advises you to uncover the complete picture. Consider the environment that you and your adversaries are in; it can divulge to you advantages you might not think possible if you only consider the strengths and weaknesses of yourself and your adversary.

22 Knowing yourself and your adversary ensures your safety. But if you want to go beyond safety and resolve the problems that will continue to trouble you, you also need to know and rely on the assistance of your environment, represented by Heaven and Ground.

The more confidence your preparations give you, the more effective your actions; the more effective your actions, the greater the chances of your success; the more successes you have, the more your confidence increases. To Sun Tzu, the ability to effect a desired outcome means careful deliberation and consistent discipline—taking the necessary time and effort—not a special skill found only in a talented few. This is good news if you don't consider yourself naturally gifted but have a strong desire to overcome the problems and conflicts in your life.

If I know the troops can attack, but do not know the enemy cannot attack, my victory is half.

If I know the enemy can be attacked, but do not know the troops cannot attack, my victory is half.

If I know the enemy can be attacked, and know the troops can attack, but do not know the ground in battle, my victory is half.[21]

Therefore, one who knows how to advance the army is limitless when taking action.

Therefore I say, if you know the enemy and know yourself, the victory is not at risk.

If you know the Heaven and you know the Ground, the victory is complete.[22]

◆ Continuing his discussion of Ground from chapter 10, Sun Tzu begins chapter 11 by defining and outlining the strategies for nine new types of ground: dispersive, marginal, contentious, open, intersecting, critical, difficult, surrounded, and deadly. A tenth type, isolated ground, is briefly discussed later in the chapter. Sun Tzu then describes strategies for unity—both disrupting it in your adversary and creating it within yourself and your supporters.

This lengthy chapter shifts from the topic of ground to unity and back to ground again with unabashed abruptness. This shifting of topics is part of the challenge of reading The Art of War, but also part of the reward, for the lesson that emerges from the interplay of these factors is how unity can facilitate the mastery of your environment and your eventual success in it.

1 The grounds listed in this verse are the nine grounds indicated by the title of the chapter. With a tenth type of ground, isolated ground, found later in the chapter, and the six grounds discussed in chapter 10, this brings the total major types of ground found in The Art of War to sixteen.

Each type has its own special characteristics worth studying, but Sun Tzu's emphasis was not on rote memorization of every nuance of each type of ground, but rather on recognizing identifiable, recurring patterns as they emerge and linking them to whatever environment you find yourself in. In fact, you could interpret the use of nine grounds to mean that there are actually countless grounds—similar to the nine changes discussed in chapter 8—that cannot be predetermined, only responded to. The nine grounds are meant to be examples of how to approach any number of different situations, rather than an exhaustive list of all possibilities.

Hence, despite its prescriptive appearance, this chapter actually calls for flexibility and adaptation to your environment and circumstances. With flexibility and adaptation you can calmly control your reactions, and thus the outcome of conflicts, without feeling the need to control the situation itself.

11 □ Nine Grounds

Sun Tzu said:

The principles of warfare are:

There are dispersive ground, marginal ground, contentious ground, open ground, intersecting ground, critical ground, difficult ground, surrounded ground, and deadly ground.[1]

(continued on page 151)

2 | This ground is called dispersive because you cause unnecessary division at home if you show the same hostility there as you would toward an outside adversary. Conflict between you and your family, friends, or others you love calls for special awareness and consideration, lest your drive to win swiftly with overwhelming force—an advantage in other situations—causes further pain and resentment, rather than reestablishing harmony.

3 | When you commit yourself only partially, you are on marginal ground. As mentioned several times previously in The Art of War, Sun Tzu did not like half-measures. Remaining close to home can become a crutch that provides support but also gives you a powerful incentive not to move forward. Being calm and comfortable in your environment is one thing, but being satisfied and lazy is another. When you're facing a conflict or an opportunity, you should be detached enough to put it in its proper perspective, but not to a point of lethargy and inaction.

4 | Contentious ground is particularly valuable because it bestows advantages on whoever occupies it first. The sunny side of high ground would be contentious ground, as it allows a small force to effectively combat a large force. Favorable environments such as contentious ground lift your morale because they enhance your strengths and minimize your weaknesses.

5 | Open ground, as previewed in chapter 8, is a double-edged sword. On one hand, open ground gives you the freedom to do what you want to do. On the other hand, your adversary has the same freedom. For example, when you are in an environment with few or lax rules, everyone is guided mainly by his or her conscience. Your ethical standards may preclude you from acting in certain ways, but unfortunately, not everyone will have such good intentions.

6 | When you enter intersecting ground, you will find many potential allies all around you. You need to befriend them to gain their support and strength. Sun Tzu believes the key lies in starting small and then building momentum. When one person begins to support and validate you, others will see it and join in.

Where the rulers do battle in their own ground, this is called dispersive ground.[2]

Where one enters the other's ground but not deep, this is called marginal ground.[3]

Where it is advantageous if you occupy it and it is advantageous if the enemy occupies it, this is called contentious ground.[4]

Where one can come and go, this is called open ground.[5]

Where ground is surrounded by others, and the first one to reach it will gain the support of the masses, this is called intersecting ground.[6]

(continued on page 153)

7 Critical ground requires utter commitment to achieve your goal. Because the army has penetrated so deeply into enemy territory that walled fortifications and cities are now behind it, it cannot reverse course or receive help from home easily. It has reached the point of no return—the only viable option is to keep moving forward. In critical ground, you are embroiled in contention with your adversary and cannot withdraw easily. You must put your full focus and effort into resolving the problem, lest you let down everyone around you, including yourself.

8 Difficult ground slows the army's movement and thus hinders its progress. You are on difficult ground when you have few options at your disposal and must slow down in order to find, analyze, and carefully choose the least harmful option. Progress toward your goal is slow, but proceeding with caution is critical to avoid even further delays.

9 Having both the features of narrow ground (difficult entry) and entrapping ground (difficult exit), surrounded ground enables a small army inside to subdue a much larger force outside. It tempers the enemy's sudden, powerful advance and continues to diminish his strength by limiting his movements and options.

For example, if an adversary has a complaint against you, you can set up a meeting to discuss the matter with him on another day (to allow a cooling period). Before the meeting, orient the two chairs next to instead of across from each other (to say, "We are not against each other, but are both on the same side"), and listen intently and ask questions (to deflate his anger by understanding its source). Although your opponent advances with great intensity, your relative position and preparation are superior to his, and so you are able to absorb and defuse the confrontation.

Where one enters deep into enemy ground, with many walled cities and towns to his back, this is called critical ground.[7]

Where there are mountains and forests, defiles and ravines, swamps and wetlands, and places difficult to pass, this is called difficult ground.[8]

Where the entrance is narrow, the exit circuitous, allowing the enemy to attack his few to our many, this is called surrounded ground.[9]

(continued on page 155)

10 Deadly ground means annihilation if soldiers don't fight. Sun Tzu believes that once soldiers are ready to die, paradoxically, they are more likely to survive because they fight more ferociously. If they fight with timidity because they fear death, they are likely to die as a consequence. In deadly ground you must employ all your energy and resources to safeguard your survival.

This sentiment was shared by seventeenth-century Japanese samurai Yamamoto Tsunetomo, as recorded in his famous book on Bushido (the traditional code of the samurai), *Hagakure:* "If by setting one's heart right every morning and evening, one is able to live as though his body is already dead, he gains freedom in the Way. His whole life will be without blame, and he will succeed in his calling."

♦ After listing each of the nine grounds and their definitions, Sun Tzu now shows how you can approach each of these nine environments in a way that allows you to avoid disaster and seize the appropriate advantage.

11 You enter dispersive ground when you engage in conflicts at home. Since the home represents your family, close friends, or even yourself, your troubles don't come from outside but from within. Sun Tzu advises you to stop contending with yourself and those who support you; you have enough contention coming from outside opponents.

12 When you partially commit on marginal ground, you also tend to hold back your efforts. You have no sense of urgency. But if your goal is worth achieving, you must stop making excuses and instead commit wholeheartedly and put all your focus, effort, and energy into achieving your goal.

Where if one who does battle with full force survives, and one who does not do battle with full force perishes, this is called deadly ground.[10]

Therefore, on dispersive ground, do not do battle.[11]

On marginal ground, do not stop.[12]

(continued on page 157)

13 Although advantageous and valuable to those who occupy it first, ground of contention has a disadvantageous effect on those who try to pursue it late. What was novel and rewarding becomes obsolete and constraining. This is Sun Tzu's way of advising you to cease striving after a goal when its appropriate time has passed. For example, a driving determination to advance in your career when you are young may be a rewarding goal, but such a singular focus once you have a family may cause misunderstanding and unhappiness at home. Is the goal still worth the price you have to pay when circumstances change?

14 Because open ground provides both the army and the enemy many ways to maneuver and attack, the army should aim for strong unity in order to create an invincible position before acting. To separate or divide would result in weakness everywhere. So, even though you have many freedoms in open ground, don't let down your guard because less scrupulous people also have many ways at their disposal to attack you.

15 Intersecting ground consists of various potential enemies and allies. Your choice is to either fight them or befriend them. Sun Tzu suggests you befriend them. You can best do this by assisting them when they need help, which shows them that they are better off alongside you than against you. One alliance will lead to another, until your overall strength surpasses your adversary's.

16 Because the army is deep behind enemy lines in critical ground, it cannot depend on supplies from home for its survival. Likewise, you must cut your dependence on the past and seek independence in order to move forward. You can sustain your progress by finding new opportunities and reaping their benefits instead of limiting yourself to what is familiar and comfortable.

On contentious ground, do not attack.[13]

On open ground, do not become separated.[14]

On intersecting ground, form alliances.[15]

On critical ground, plunder.[16]

(continued on page 159)

17 Tough circumstances can wear you down. You may find yourself in an environment where the difficulties seem overwhelming. Sun Tzu advises you to press on through the difficulties, because you can best alleviate your hardships by moving forward instead of lingering in your misery. You cannot avoid hardships, but you can reduce your time in them.

18 With its narrow opening and circuitous exit, surrounded ground resembles a trap. When you must enter surrounded ground, Sun Tzu suggests you prepare yourself by building strength to counter the high risks and limit your losses should you face calamity.

19 Deadly ground may cause you to feel fear and angst, but it also inspires you to give your best effort since you have so much to lose. You contend not only for your own survival, but also for the survival of those who depend on you for their safety and livelihood.

♦ Although Sun Tzu seems to have concluded his discussion of the grounds, he returns to them later in the chapter. Now he turns his attention to the subject of unity: how to disrupt it in your adversary and how to build it within yourself and those around you.

20 By appealing to what were "ancient times" even to him, Sun Tzu aptly demonstrates the timelessness of the human tendency to think mostly about our own self-interests, instead of the interests of the whole group. If you can skillfully stimulate this tendency in your adversary, Sun Tzu says you will be able to divide him and his supporters, thereby weakening him and discouraging him from continuing the fight.

21 While increasing your strength through unity (being "assembled"), you can simultaneously disrupt your adversary's unity (cause them to be "separated and unable to assemble"). You remain strong to defend yourself while rendering your adversary harmless. When you dash his hopes and make yourself unconquerable, he himself becomes more open to negotiations. With no other favorable options, it is in his best interest to seek peace.

On difficult ground, press on.[17]

On surrounded ground, be prepared.[18]

On deadly ground, do battle.[19]

In ancient times, those skilled in warfare were able to prevent the unity of the enemy's front and back, the many and the few, the noble and the peasants, and the superiors and the subordinates.[20]

Have the enemy be separated and unable to assemble;

if the enemy is assembled, it should not be organized.[21]

(continued on page 161)

22 Sun Tzu affirms that not taking action can require the same amount of contemplation, intentionality, and discipline as taking action. When you understand your limits, you understand that doing something at an inopportune time can do more damage than if you had simply left things alone.

23 When you ascertain what your opponent truly cares about, you can influence his or her future actions, despite an inequality in position or strength.

24 In this context, *speed* does not simply mean "moving fast," but rather reacting to changing conditions swiftly and effectively. When you are quicker in adjusting to your environment than your adversary, you are more prepared and thus gain the upper hand. In this way, superior numbers may prove irrelevant, or even burdensome.

25 Sun Tzu promotes the care of the body because he understands its effect on your frame of mind. To him, preserving your physical vitality enables you to maintain your internal balance and harmony, even in the midst of external chaos and conflict.

Move when advantageous, stop when not advantageous.[22]

Ask:

If the enemy is large in number and advances, what should be the response?

I say:

Seize what he values, and he will do what you wish.[23]

The essential factor in warfare is speed.

To take advantage of the enemy's lack of preparation, take unexpected routes to attack where the enemy is not prepared.[24]

Generally, the Way of invading is when one has penetrated deep into enemy ground, and the troops are united;

the defender will not be able to prevail.

If you plunder the fertile fields, the army will have enough provisions.

If you take care of your health, avoid fatigue, you will be united, and will build strength.[25]

(continued on page 163)

26 Instinctively, soldiers will choose what is most favorable to them. If they have to choose between dying and fighting, they will fight. Only when they face real danger will they work hard and exert their full strength.

If you are truly wise, you won't wait for an emergency to create a sense of urgency or clarify your priorities. A traditional Buddhist verse sometimes uttered at the end of a meditation session similarly reminds us of the crucial importance of focus and full commitment in every moment of our lives:

> Let me respectfully remind you:
> Life and death are of supreme importance.
> Time passes swiftly by and opportunity is lost.
> Each of us should strive to awaken, awaken.
> Awaken! Take heed. Do not squander your life.

27 Rather than trying to manipulate people directly, a skilled general determines the conditions, and then lets people act freely within those conditions. Knowing they will act according to their own best interests given their situation, he can accurately predict and solicit the behavior he wants, while still allowing people to make their own decisions.

28 In ancient China, as well as in most of the ancient world, people relied on soothsayers and fortune-telling to predict outcomes of future events.

Sun Tzu offers a better, more practical solution: prohibit omens altogether. You can best predict your future by controlling it yourself, not by trusting luck or fate to control it. When you compare your ability with the ability of your adversary and make the most out of your environment, you can have no doubt about who will prevail. This formula isn't mystical or magical—it is entirely practical and down-to-earth. A similar prohibition is found in the Hebrew Bible: "Do not turn to mediums or wizards; do not seek them out" (Leviticus 19:31). Trusting such dubious practices dilutes your reliance on your true source of power.

When moving troops and calculating plans, be formless.

Throw your troops into situations where there is no escape, where they will die before escaping.

When they are about to die, what can they not do?

They will exert their full strength.

When the troops are in desperate situations, they fear nothing;

having penetrated deep in enemy ground, they are united.

When there are no other alternatives, they will fight.[26]

Therefore, though not disciplined, they are alert;

though not asked, they are devoted;

though without promises, they are faithful;

and though not commanded, they are trustworthy.[27]

Prohibit omens, and get rid of doubts, and they will die without any other thoughts.[28]

(continued on page 165)

29 The challenge is to address people's natural propensity to avoid conflict or danger in hopes of securing a long and prosperous life. You yourself might prefer to do what is most safe and comfortable instead of struggling in tough and risky situations. Who would not? However, when you encounter an imminent conflict that you cannot (and should not) avoid, you have no choice but to face it. The wise course is to risk a certain amount of loss by confronting the situation immediately, rather than allowing the problem to fester until it grows to unmanageable proportions and causes true devastation.

30 Chuan Chu and Ts'ao Kuei were legendary for their brave acts. In 515 BCE, Chuan Chu hid a dagger inside a fish and used it to kill the king of the Wu state, Wang Liao, in front of numerous dinner guests. Sun Tzu mentions this story because it happened close to the time of his presentation of The Art of War to King Ho Lu. It was also fitting because Chuan Chu was sent on this mission by none other than Ho Lu himself!

In 681 BCE, Ts'ao Kuei, a government minister from the defeated Lu state, held Huan Kung, duke of the victor state, Ch'i, at knife point during a treaty negotiation. The duke's armed bodyguards, shocked by the incident unfolding before their eyes, didn't dare move. Ts'ao Kuei demanded fair dealing for his Lu state, instead of Huan Kung's one-sided proposals, and Huan Kung had no choice but to acquiesce. Ts'ao Kuei then threw down his knife and tried to continue the meeting. Understandably, Huan Kung balked, but Ts'ao Kuei steadfastly invoked the honor of his words, and the duke reluctantly proceeded with the negotiations.

Incurring great risks to their own safety, both Chuan Chu and Ts'ao Kuei threw themselves into perilous situations in order to promote their causes. Their courage seems beyond reproach. More important, their courage helped them to achieve their aims. When it comes to your aims and goals, do you value them enough to display similar courage?

The soldiers do not have wealth, but not because they dislike material goods;

they do not live long, but not because they dislike longevity.

On the day the men are issued orders to do battle, the sitting soldiers' tears will soak their sleeves, and the lying soldiers' tears will roll down their cheeks.[29]

However, if you throw them into a desperate situation, they will have the courage of Chuan Chu or Ts'ao Kuei.[30]

(continued on page 167)

31 In this verse, Sun Tzu elucidates two ideas. First, unity of purpose and flexibility are superior to brute force. Similar to a *shuaijan,* you can respond quickly to negate your adversary's advances, no matter where he or she attacks. Second, even bitter enemies such as the Wu and Yueh states can join together if they share the same plight and are "in the same boat." Despite your involvement in a bitter conflict, you can try to identify common ground between you and your enemy. With this act, you create a potential opportunity to disarm your adversary and reach an amicable agreement.

32 Hobbling horses and burying chariots inhibit soldiers from retreating. However, according to Sun Tzu, that is still insufficient. The general must also place his soldiers in environments such as critical ground, deep in enemy territory, where they naturally unite due to the vast dangers all around them.

Though you probably won't place people in peril for their actual lives, you can find ways of placing them in urgent situations where they can unite. Whether this is working to meet a critical deadline or planning an important upcoming event, desperate situations make people put aside their petty differences, come together, and help one another in a common cause.

33 By deliberately preventing his soldiers from knowing the overall strategy, a general frees them from the worries and complexities he faces as a leader. He wants them to concentrate fully on their individual duties, for if they fail at their small tasks, the overall strategy that depends on those tasks will also fail. The Buddhist concept of *samadhi* exemplifies a similar kind of total concentration, during which the person focuses his or her mind on one object until an insight occurs. This attention to detail is important in life today as well; if you keep your eyes on the big picture but fail to execute the individual steps, you aren't likely to reach your goal.

Therefore, those skilled in warfare are like the *shuaijan*.

The *shuaijan* is a serpent on Mount Chang.

If you strike its head, its tail attacks;

if you strike its tail, its head attacks;

if you strike its middle, both the head and tail attack.

Ask:

Can forces be made like the *shuaijan*?

I say:

They can.

The men of Wu and Yueh hated each other, however, encountering severe winds when crossing a river on the same boat, they assisted each other like left and right hands.[31]

Therefore, hobbling horses and burying chariot wheels are not enough.

The Way of organization is uniting their courage, making the best of the strong and the weak through the principles of Ground.

Therefore, one who is skilled in warfare leads them by the hand like they are one person;

they cannot but follow.[32]

It is important for a general to be calm and remote, upright and disciplined, and able to mystify his men's eyes and ears, keeping them ignorant.

He changes his methods and plans, keeping them from knowing.

He changes his campsites and takes circuitous routes, keeping them from anticipating.[33]

(continued on page 169)

34 The job of the general is to lead soldiers into battle where nothing less than the utmost commitment, focus, and strength of every soldier is required for survival. Holding back in the hope of retreating to a pre-confrontation status quo will lead to catastrophe. When the time comes to confront your adversary or problem, you must relinquish all hope of returning to the status quo and instead press forward with all your might for a solution.

Sun Tzu mentions "troops ... herded to and fro without them knowing where they are going." Since the soldiers are focused on their singular task, not the whole operation or entire strategy, they can be "herded to and fro" because they truly trust that the general knows what he is doing and is keeping the army's safety and well-being (see annotation 41 later in this chapter) in mind.

♦ Sun Tzu returns to his discussion of grounds from earlier in the chapter, presenting the ideas again but from a different strategic angle. He will then finish the chapter by turning once again to the topic of unity.

Some scholars surmise this chapter's awkward organization was caused by an unintentional jumbling of the order of the bamboo slips on which The Art of War was inscribed. Whatever the case, one result of this organization is that a potentially monotonous discourse of the many types of ground is broken into more digestible segments.

35 Again Sun Tzu refers to human nature and tendency in conflicts. As much as you would like to think you base your decisions purely on logic, sentiments often influence your actions. Becoming keenly aware of your own emotional state, and the state of those around you, helps you to control your own actions and influence the actions of others. Likewise, observing the emotions of your adversary allows you to use those emotions to guide him or her away from causing you harm.

36 Isolated ground is the only ground not part of the nine grounds in this chapter. The solitary description of it is apropos in both description and context.

The day the general leads his troops into battle, it is like climbing up high and throwing away the ladder.

He leads his troops deep into enemy ground, and releases the trigger.

He burns his boats and destroys the cooking pots.

He commands his troops like herding sheep;

being herded to and fro without them knowing where they are going.

Assembling the masses of the army, and throwing them into danger are the responsibility of the general.[34]

Adaptations to the nine grounds, the advantages in defensive and offensive maneuvers, and the patterns of human emotions must be examined.[35]

Generally, the Way of invading is:

When troops are deep in enemy ground, they are united;

when troops are not deep in enemy ground, they are scattered.

Where you leave your country, and lead the troops across the border into enemy ground, this is called isolated ground.[36]

(continued on page 171)

37 Sun Tzu largely repeats the definitions of previously mentioned grounds. Scholars have long speculated why he does this. One possibility is that he does it for mnemonic purposes. These one-liners serve as pithy reminders of the chief characteristics of each of the nine grounds.

38 You're on marginal ground when you enter your adversary's domain, but not deeply. About this ground, Sun Tzu said previously, "Do not stop." Here, Sun Tzu also suggests that you should consolidate your support because you want everyone to put forth all their effort and commitment to the goal. Because of momentum, no one person can hesitate and go back if everyone else moves forward.

39 You gain advantage on contentious ground when you occupy it first. Sun Tzu said earlier, "Do not attack [if you lose that advantage]." He also advises you to hurry because lingering prevents you from occupying that environment first.

40 On intersecting ground, you gain the support of others when you arrive first. Sun Tzu previously said, "Form alliances." Seeking new allies helps to augment your strength, but strengthening your existing alliances is equally important because losing one will cancel out any new alliance you may forge.

41 Some past commentators interpreted this verse to mean that Sun Tzu advocates purposely blocking soldiers' escape routes in order to throw them into a desperate situation. However, this interpretation means the general would be putting his soldiers at a distinct and unnecessary disadvantage: throwing them in danger makes them want to unite, but the narrowness of surrounded ground prevents them from uniting as a whole and operating at full strength. The troops would not survive with such a severe handicap. In accord with The Art of War's general theme of safety and advantage, a more likely reading is that Sun Tzu intended to block the *enemy's* openings. The enemy soldiers now would have no choice but to continue down the narrow and circuitous path where they would be at a clear disadvantage.

Where there are four sides open, this is called intersecting ground.

Where you penetrated deep in enemy ground, this is called critical ground.

Where you penetrated little in enemy ground, this is called marginal ground.

Where the back is impassable and the front is narrow, this is called surrounded ground.

Where there is nowhere to go, this is called deadly ground.[37]

Therefore, on dispersive ground, I have my troops united.

On marginal ground, I consolidate my troops.[38]

On contentious ground, I hurry my back.[39]

On open ground, I pay attention to our defenses.

On intersecting ground, I strengthen our alliances.[40]

On critical ground, I maintain continuous supply of provisions.

On difficult ground, I press on quickly.

On surrounded ground, I block off openings.[41]

(continued on page 173)

42 On deadly ground, you survive if you take action with full force. Sun Tzu earlier said, "Do battle," when on deadly ground. When you demonstrate to people the problems they will face and the urgency needed to face those problems, you get their attention. The word *our* in this verse is important because it signifies that everyone has the same goal and will stay united, even through great danger.

43 Navigating effectively through the nine grounds—indeed, through any type of ground—depends on intimate knowledge of your circumstances. If you don't have firsthand knowledge of your situation, seek those who do. To Sun Tzu, firsthand knowledge is crucial. You cannot accept anything less accurate and reliable, especially when your very survival is at stake. With knowledge, you move with speed because you take action without hesitation and without making unnecessary mistakes.

♦ Sun Tzu ends his discussion on ground and now finishes the chapter by once again taking up the concept of unity.

44 Some readers may erroneously interpret this verse to mean that you don't need to form alliances, but this was not Sun Tzu's intent. When you show overwhelming force from the beginning, your adversary doesn't have the time or unity of purpose to form alliances. As if you were on intersecting ground, the momentum of acquiring more allies starts with your initial show of strength, which signals your superiority to your potential allies. Therefore, you won't need to contend with your adversary for alliances, since potential allies will naturally gravitate to you.

45 Every ally that supports you means one fewer supporter for your enemy. In time, you can gain enough allies that your collective strength can overwhelm the most powerful of adversaries, and simultaneously lighten your own share of the burden.

On deadly ground, I show the troops our resolve to fight to the death.

Therefore, the nature of the army is:

To defend when surrounded, to fight hard when there are no other alternatives, and to obey commands promptly when in danger.[42]

Therefore, one who does not know the intentions of the rulers of the neighboring states cannot secure alliances.

One who does not know the mountains and forests, gorges and defiles, swamps and wetlands cannot advance the army.

One who does not use local guides cannot take advantage of the ground.

One who does not know any one of these matters cannot command the army of a ruler.[43]

When the army of a ruler attacks a great nation, the nation's masses cannot assemble.

When its power overwhelms the nation, alliances cannot be formed.

Therefore, one does not contend with alliances of other nations.[44]

One does not foster the power of other nations.

If one pursues his aims, overwhelming the enemy, then he can take the enemy's cities and overthrow kingdoms.[45]

(continued on page 175)

46 Consistent with the nine changes discussed in chapter 8, Sun Tzu shows his dislike of rigid rules. Rules can serve as guidelines for general situations, but a unique situation should not be strictly dictated by them. In this verse he encourages you to take extraordinary steps that befit extraordinary circumstances. Don't be hindered by mundane, irrelevant rules from taking the action you need to take.

47 In this verse, Sun Tzu encapsulates the two main concepts of this chapter: taking advantage of ground and creating unity. Sun Tzu values the contribution of his soldiers and wants to make certain each does his part without the worries of anything else. Soldiers who put forth their best effort progress to face great danger and land on deadly ground. But they will survive because they will unite and each do his small part, adding up to the smooth execution of the general's grand strategy. What seems like imminent defeat can result in effortless victory.

Likewise, when you are faced with a pressing predicament, the enormity of your problem can confuse and overwhelm you. In this situation, consolidate your strength and focus on what you can do immediately. By concentrating on the immediate tasks and completing them in succession, you chip away at your problem until you eventually overcome it. As Sun Tzu said in chapter 9, "It is enough to consolidate your strength, calculate the enemy, and get support from your men." In other words, you don't need to formulate complicated strategies to solve complicated conflicts. Execute simple strategies well, and it will be sufficient.

48 Don't merely react to the actions of your adversary—learn his intentions before he does anything, by gathering information from people who are close to him. Sun Tzu calls these people spies and discusses them in detail in chapter 13, "Using Spies."

Give out rewards transcending law, give out commands transcending policy.[46]

Command the masses like commanding one person.

Give your troops tasks, but do not reveal your plans to them.

Get them to face danger, but do not reveal the advantages.

Throw them into danger and they will survive;

put them on deadly ground and they will live.

Only if the troops are in situations of danger will they turn defeat into victory.[47]

The concern of warfare is that operations are in accord with the enemy's intentions.[48]

(continued on page 177)

49 When you know your adversary's intentions, you know exactly what to do—what to concentrate on and what not to concentrate on—even if you're a great distance away. The actions you take that people describe as having extraordinary "wit and skill," as if you're clairvoyant, are in reality, backed by ordinary, reliable information.

50 Going to war requires total commitment and sometimes drastic measures—both offensive, in committing resources and troops, and defensive, in ensuring the safety of your territory from attack. Therefore, the decision to go to war should not be made in haste but with utmost seriousness and patient contemplation, as if regarding the matter in the quiet spaciousness of a temple. For Sun Tzu, there was no such thing as a casual war or a war that did not involve sacrifice.

51 As illustrated by the nine grounds discussed in this chapter, your approach changes whenever your environment changes. Flexibility is the key to victory, for fixed size and strength can quickly become irrelevant, even a liability, in a rapidly changing environment.

52 Some people understand the way of warfare as entailing brute force, but Sun Tzu views it as a matter of intention, purpose, and skill—like an enticing maiden who lures the enemy into a vulnerable position and then acts as swiftly as a hare to pacify him. The result is the same—victory—but the means involve little force. This image of achieving victory without violence resonates with one of Sun Tzu's most-quoted verses, "To subjugate the enemy's army without doing battle is the highest of excellence" (see chapter 3), which could only come from a mature mind that values both intelligence and compassion, even in as senseless and violent an activity as war.

If one then concentrates his strength on the enemy, killing his general a thousand *li* away, this is called achieving objectives through wit and skill.[49]

Therefore, on the day war is declared, close off all borders, destroy all passports, and do not allow their envoys to pass.

Go through your plans in the temple and bring about the execution of those plans.[50]

If the enemy presents an opportunity, take advantage of it.

Attack what he values most.

Do not advance on any fixed day or time;

calculate and adapt to the enemy to determine the matter of doing battle.[51]

Therefore, be like a maiden;

once the enemy opens the door, be like a scurrying hare.

The enemy will be unable to prevail.[52]

◆ Fire attacks are specialized and highly destructive attacks on what your adversary values most. Sun Tzu picks fire instead of other types of weapons, because it is readily available, even if the army lacks other resources. He begins this chapter by defining five kinds of fire attacks and then proposes five ways or possibilities of starting a fire and benefiting from it. He also warns about the inherent dangers in using fire attacks, and reiterates his central point that such attacks are not intended to destroy for the sake of destruction, but to hasten the end of the conflict. Given their supreme potency, not a single spark should be lit without first having that goal in mind.

1 "Burning personnel" does not mean literally burning soldiers, but burning the buildings they are in, to drive them out. (Given the limited technologies Sun Tzu had, burning soldiers themselves in any practical manner would not have been possible.) Burning an enemy's housing, provisions, equipment, stores, weapons, and other prized possessions causes them to panic and act hastily, thus exposing their vulnerabilities or, ideally, causing them to lose the will to continue fighting altogether.

In everyday conflicts, a common way to inflame your adversary is to attack his ego or reputation, a prized possession for many people, spurring him to respond in a rash manner. As a result, he loses the focus of his original objective and becomes sidetracked, while you calmly race ahead to outmaneuver and render him harmless. Your intent is not to revel in this apparent manipulation of another person, even though he is your adversary, but to disrupt his focus, redirect his anger, and delay his plans to do you harm.

12 □ Fire Attacks

Sun Tzu said:

There are five kinds of fire attacks:

One, burning personnel;

two, burning provisions;

three, burning equipment;

four, burning stores;

five, burning weapons.[1]

(*continued on page 181*)

2 For a fire attack to work, conditions must be conducive for fire to burn—literally or figuratively. Sun Tzu goes on to describe what these conditions are for the battlefield. For your purposes, you must be sure that an adversary is vulnerable to such attacks, such as being sufficiently arrogant. An overly proud person doesn't like to have his or her faults pointed out, and so will react harshly and recklessly. Having "equipment ... available beforehand" also means planning carefully to see the attack through because, by provoking an arrogant person, you are certainly "playing with fire."

3 The four days Sun Tzu mentions are when the moon aligns with the constellations Sagittarius (Chi), Andromeda (Pi), Crater (I), and Corvus (Chen). Even though we no longer watch the moon and stars to predict changes in the weather, the concept of anticipating the appropriate time for an attack still applies. Similar to waiting for the right seasons, moon phases, or rising winds, if you wait until your adversary's haughtiness is piqued, any slight against his or her reputation is likely to provoke a predictable response.

4 Sun Tzu discusses five changes of fire, or the five possibilities to commence an incendiary attack, and what to do afterward. You can use these as guidelines as you approach and manage provocation.

The first possibility is to surround and contain the fire. When you provoke your adversary directly, be ready to adapt quickly to his or her response. If your adversary reacts in a sudden burst of anger, ensure you have sufficient strength to remain calm and carefully observe any weaknesses he or she exposes during the outburst. This is remaining formless while you determine your adversary's form. You will learn what weakness you can attack with your strength.

5 The second possibility is to remain patient and flexible. Not all your opponents will respond with anger immediately. Your adversary might not appear upset initially but will respond eventually to protect her ego. Your patience allows you to stay alert until the moment when she takes action.

Using fire attacks depends on proper conditions.

Equipment for fire attacks must be available beforehand.[2]

There are appropriate seasons for using fire attacks, and appropriate days for raising fires.

The appropriate season is when the weather is dry;

the appropriate day is when the moon is at Chi, Pi, I, or Chen.

These four days are when there are rising winds.[3]

Generally, in fire attacks, you must respond according to the five changes of fire:

If the fires are set inside enemy camp, you must respond quickly outside the enemy camp;[4]

if the fires are set but the enemy is calm, then wait, do not attack.[5]

(continued on page 183)

6 The third possibility is to resist fanning the flames unnecessarily and instead let your adversary's arrogance fuel his anger. Remain patient to allow the pressure to build, and force the adversary to take action. "Follow up if you can" means responding to him once he loses emotional control. "Stay if you cannot" means remaining vigilant while you wait to ascertain how your adversary will respond. Just as you carefully watch the progression of an actual fire that you set, observe the unfolding events with great care and caution.

7 The fourth possibility is to set the fire around the perimeter, as opposed to the inside. This is analogous to provoking your adversary indirectly, via another person. "When the time is right" means ensuring the message you're sending gets through to your adversary.

8 The fifth and final possibility of attack by fire is to set the fire upwind. An able general doesn't set fires upwind and attack downwind because he will be trapped between the fire behind him and the enemy ahead of him. This kind of poor planning wouldn't allow him to maneuver in either direction. Instead, he sets the fire ahead of him and attacks after the fire draws out the enemy.

Likewise, use caution when employing attacks on your adversary's reputation, lest you get burned by your own words. For example, unless people understand your overall intent or the reasonable cause of your attacks, they may think you callous or worse, and you may lose their trust and support. Communicate first with your allies and potential allies before taking action.

9 Just as winds rise and fall, your adversary's mood is sure to change. He or she may feel infallible one moment, but cautious the next, and your attacks may elicit a range of reactions, including ire, panic, or ambivalence. Know when one emotion ends and another starts.

Let the fire reach its height, and follow up if you can, stay if you cannot;[6]

If the fire attack can be set outside, without relying on the inside, set it when the time is right.[7]

If the fire is set upwind, do not attack downwind.[8]

If it is windy all during the day, the wind will stop at night.[9]

(continued on page 185)

10 The water Sun Tzu refers to here was mentioned in chapter 9, regarding dividing an army by crossing a river. Water or the crossing of a river represents division that leaves the army vulnerable. If you have sufficient power or strength, you can employ water by dividing your opponents and separating them from their supporters, thus weakening them.

When you are weaker than your opponent and low on resources, you don't have sufficient strength to use water. Fire, however, is readily available to anyone—but distracting your adversaries with fire attacks demands extraordinary intelligence and skill in dealing with the necessary careful timing and inherent danger.

Neither water nor fire can be used to plunder in the literal sense; Sun Tzu is alluding to the destructive nature of fire. This reference to fire and plundering was mentioned in chapter 7, where the army—like fire—sweeps through the enemy land with ferocious intensity.

11 While Sun Tzu talks about the dangers of overreaction, he also warns against being too cautious and not responding quickly enough in times of opportunity. So whereas arrogance leaves you vulnerable, pessimism makes you hesitate. Often, by the time you realize you need to act, the opportunity has already passed. Wisdom enables you to evaluate the possibilities, but decisive action is also necessary if you want to achieve your goals swiftly.

12 True to his nature, Sun Tzu wraps up the chapter by emphasizing the importance of remembering the ultimate goal: to end the conflict quickly and peaceably. Do not start a fire just to start a fire and make matters worse. Identify the actual benefit and consider the total cost of your actions before taking any of them.

The army must know the five changes of fire, to be able to calculate the appropriate days.

Those who use fire to assist in attacks are intelligent, those who use water to assist in attacks are powerful.

Water can be used to cut off the enemy, but cannot be used to plunder.[10]

If one gains victory in battle and is successful in attacks, but does not exploit those achievements, it is disastrous.

This is called waste and delay.

Therefore, I say the wise general thinks about it, and the good general executes it.[11]

If it is not advantageous, do not move;

if there is no gain, do not use troops;

if there is no danger, do not do battle.[12]

(continued on page 187)

13 As you would cause your adversary to do something careless, others may try to do the same to you. Sun Tzu reminds you that no matter how angry you feel, like the seasons, winds, moon, and constellations, your moods will change. Your ego, although bruised, can heal again, but if you act out in anger, you can do irreparable damage, such as losing the trust of your supporters. Resorting to devastating fire attacks to assuage feelings of vengeance or fear will only create more profound problems later on.

14 In this verse, Sun Tzu emphasizes the advantages of prudence and caution, which provide a foundation of safety and security for the nation and its people. Recklessly charging ahead can easily result in setbacks. Interestingly, as explored throughout this chapter, the dangers that set you back often originate not from your enemy, but from within your own emotional self. By understanding and controlling your emotions, you can start to understand and control many of your dangers.

The ruler may not move his army out of anger;

the general may not do battle out of wrath.

If it is advantageous, move;

if it is not advantageous, stop.

Those angry will be happy again, and those wrathful will be cheerful again, but a destroyed nation cannot exist again, the dead cannot be brought back to life.[13]

Therefore, the enlightened ruler is prudent, the good general is cautious.

This is the Way of securing the nation, and preserving the army.[14]

◆ This controversial chapter about spies doesn't warrant the suspicion it sometimes receives. As in the rest of The Art of War, the methods Sun Tzu discusses are not devious ends in themselves. Rather, they are ways of effectively gathering and managing relevant information from people who have intimate knowledge of your adversary with the purpose of ending your conflict with him or her quickly and, hopefully, peaceably. Such people with privileged information are often called spies, and this word often connotes a self-centered betrayal of principle and the backstabbing of trusted friends. From Sun Tzu's perspective, however, spies are those who are aligned with a greater purpose and are willing to put themselves at risk in order to accelerate progress in stopping war and possibly saving a multitude of lives.

1 Just like wars today, wars in Sun Tzu's time were costly endeavors that took a heavy financial toll on the people and the nation. This verse reiterates the idea first introduced in chapter 2, that due to its enormous cost, you should only choose to enter a confrontation as a last resort.

2 For every Chinese soldier sent into battle, seven families had to labor to support him. Thus, the toll of war wasn't only economic—the entire nation endured strain whenever it declared war. Likewise, conflict doesn't always involve only you and your adversary but affects other people close to you as well. When you feel pain, those who care for you feel it, too. So when you end a conflict, you also end the suffering of many people directly and indirectly involved.

3 With the countless hours and vast amounts of resources poured into the preparation for a single day of battle, the pressure on each army to succeed intensifies exponentially. Unfortunately, success in this case means leaving the battlefield with fewer deaths than the other side. The process can best be described as preparing for a large mass funeral. Implied in Sun Tzu's observation is the belief that this type of battle borders on madness.

13 □ Using Spies

Sun Tzu said:

Generally, raising an army of a hundred thousand and advancing it a thousand *li*, the expenses to the people and the nation's resources are one thousand gold pieces a day.[1]

Those in commotion internally and externally, those exhausted on the roads, and those unable to do their daily work are seven hundred thousand families.[2]

Two sides remain in standoff for several years in order to do battle for a decisive victory on a single day.[3]

(continued on page 191)

4 What *is* madness is refusing to find a simpler, less costly, and less destructive way of settling conflict. According to Sun Tzu, one more intelligent way of doing battle involves obtaining foreknowledge, which depends on reliable information about the enemy—his intention, condition, and location. With this knowledge, the general can thwart the enemy's strategies instead of killing his enemy's soldiers, or thwart the enemy's movements instead of allowing the enemy to outmaneuver him and kill his soldiers. Therefore, given the enormous costs of preparing for war, including the waste and devastation of waged battles, the cost of obtaining reliable information is the last thing a general should worry about. If he refuses to procure information, then he values a few gold coins more than people's lives. This, indeed, is the height of inhumanity.

5 To Sun Tzu, foreknowledge doesn't rely on the supernatural but on practical, firsthand reports of the situation. These may not be as exciting as mysterious signs or obscure divinations, but their very mundaneness is what ensures success: no amount of esoteric speculation can predict an outcome as well as direct, empirical observation of the enemy's strengths and weaknesses. With hard evidence, your decisions will be sound and the results will be predictable.

Yet refusing to outlay a hundred pieces of gold, and thereby not knowing the enemy's situation, is the height of inhumanity.

This one is not the general of the people, a help to the ruler, or the master of victory.

What enables the enlightened rulers and good generals to conquer the enemy at every move and achieve extraordinary success is foreknowledge.[4]

Foreknowledge cannot be elicited from ghosts and spirits;

it cannot be inferred from comparison of previous events, or from the calculations of the heavens, but must be obtained from people who have knowledge of the enemy's situation.[5]

(continued on page 193)

6 You may feel uncomfortable with the idea of using spies to obtain information because spies employ deceit and even betrayal. And yet, if you can go beyond the superficial labels, such strategies can be employed for the greater good. Consider how infiltrating gangs or crime rings with informants—spies—helps law enforcement bring criminals to justice more swiftly. These informants are simply individuals who have the firsthand knowledge you need to make informed decisions.

"No one knows their Way" means no one (especially your enemy) knows the relationship you have with your spies. Because they provide intimate knowledge of your adversary, you can act with extraordinary accuracy and precision against your adversary, as if you derive your skill from the supernatural or divine guidance.

7 Local spies are acquaintances of your adversary. Internal spies are close friends or family members of your adversary. Double spies are those whom your adversary believes are reporting on you, but who have actually turned and are serving you. Dead spies are your own agents who spread false information about you; they help you to remain formless. These spies are called dead because you cannot use them again once people realize the information they spread is false. Living spies are your own agents who actively gather information about your adversary. Each type of spy has a valuable role to play in your noble cause.

Therefore there are five kinds of spies used:

Local spies, internal spies, double spies, dead spies, and living spies.

When all five are used, and no one knows their Way, it is called the divine organization, and is the ruler's treasure.[6]

For local spies, we use the enemy's people.

For internal spies, we use the enemy's officials.

For double spies, we use the enemy's spies.

For dead spies we use agents to spread misinformation to the enemy. For living spies, we use agents to return with reports.[7]

(continued on page 195)

8 When compared to the emotional and tangible costs of conflicts, obtaining information that can curtail those costs will be worth your time and effort. Therefore, remain close to your spies. Instead of only calling upon them when you need them, continually build a strong bond with them and help them whenever they need assistance. If you don't have informants who are close to your enemy, you need to seek them out. Earn their trust and build the same tight-knit relationship with them as you do with your existing spies.

Secrecy in this verse relates to the formlessness you must maintain in your relationship with each of your spies. Without formlessness your spy may be exposed, and your enemy will be unlikely to share any more information with him.

9 Using the five types of spies is not an exercise in curiosity or an intriguing power struggle but a practical way for you and your opponent to stop incurring further losses. Without your benevolent intentions, your spies may refuse to support your cause and turn against you. If they turn against you, they can serve as double spies for your adversary. Only if you are aware of your spies' subtle cues and motives will you be able to distinguish between those who are loyal to you and those who may be double spies for the enemy.

Sun Tzu implies in this verse that information doesn't always equate with usable knowledge. You may have numerous briefings with your spies, but how valuable are they if they don't make sense or are even contradictory? You must have the wisdom and discernment to understand how each piece of the puzzle fits (is truthful, unbiased, and relevant)—or doesn't fit (is untruthful, biased, and irrelevant)—into a coherent whole. This can be a tricky task—"subtle, subtle!" Sun Tzu called it.

10 To say you have too many spies is like saying you know too many people. The more people you know, the more opportunities you have to learn about what you don't understand. And the more you understand, the better your foreknowledge of every situation you enter.

Therefore, of those close to the army, none is closer than spies, no reward more generously given, and no matter in greater secrecy.[8]

Only the wisest ruler can use spies;

only the most benevolent and upright general can use spies, and only the most alert and observant person can get the truth using spies.

It is subtle, subtle![9]

There is nowhere that spies cannot be used.[10]

(continued on page 197)

11 If one of your spies becomes compromised, your whole web of informants could unravel. By today's standards, Sun Tzu's solution may seem barbaric, but you must remember that the conflicts he wrote about involved the lives of entire nations. In most modern applications, the verse's advice to "put to death" those who know about your compromised spies' activities means you should break ties with your spies and those involved, since you could put yourself and them at further risk.

12 Information is paramount. It is the key that lets you penetrate your adversary's seemingly invincible position. Like a magic trick revealed, what might have looked impossible before now looks quite simple. Even if you are the weaker side, you start to perceive ways to negate your weaknesses and accentuate your strengths based on your adversary's revealed strengths and weaknesses.

Sun Tzu lays out a comprehensive plan for achieving maximum knowledge about your adversary while simultaneously maintaining formlessness for yourself. The linchpin in the plan begins with winning over enemy spies to help you lay the groundwork for your own network of espionage. Although spies in general deserve your attention, double spies—those close to your adversary but who also serve you— demand your full commitment. Once you gain their trust, they will support you in return. Double spies are most valuable to you because they have firsthand knowledge of your adversary, can identify enemy spies seeking information about you, and can prevent your opponent from ascertaining your position. Thus, double spies serve both as your advocates and protectors.

If a spy's activities are leaked before they are to begin, the spy and those who know should be put to death.[11]

Generally, if you want to attack an army, besiege a walled city, assassinate individuals, you must know the identities of the defending generals, assistants, associates, gate guards, and officers.

You must have spies seek and learn them.

You must seek enemy spies.[12]

(continued on page 199)

13 Through the intimate knowledge of your enemy gained by your double spies, you learn where and how to recruit local and internal spies. From their knowledge, you learn the best way to disseminate misinformation through your dead spies, and can screen the activities of your living spies.

In the previous verse and this one, Sun Tzu's intricate discussion of building and maintaining a spy network may seem daunting. But, as we'll explore further in the next verse, none of these relationships can work without the moral approval of everyone involved. It is the bond that holds the network together. Therefore, your cause must be noble and your aim must be benevolent, or the bond will break. This requirement applies as much to you as to your enemy.

14 I Chih was a minister to the malicious final ruler of the Hsia dynasty (2205–1766 BCE); Lu Ya was a minister in the subsequent Yin dynasty (1766–1045 BCE). I Chih helped overthrow the Hsia dynasty and give rise to the first and honorable emperor of the Yin dynasty; Lu Ya helped put an end to the last and corrupt emperor of that same Yin dynasty. Both of these men had the sagacity to abandon their malevolent superiors and side with those who were benevolent to them and to the people of China.

When you take action that is in the best interest of others, you engender support and loyalty. When you use your resources for selfish motives, those who would support you, such as your spies, soon abandon you for your adversary.

15 With this last verse in The Art of War, we come full circle to the first chapter, "Calculations." By yourself, you can calculate your own advantages and disadvantages with regard to the five main factors of conflict: Way, Heaven, Ground, General, and Law. Now, with the intelligence gathered from spies, you have the same intimate knowledge about your opponent as you do about yourself and you can complete the assessment of your enemy's strengths and weaknesses in the same five factors. With this panoramic view of your world, how can you not succeed in overcoming your conflict?

Bribe them, and instruct and retain them.

Therefore, double spies can be obtained and used.

From their knowledge, you can obtain local and internal spies.

From their knowledge, the dead spies can spread misinformation to the enemy.

From their knowledge, our living spies can be used as planned.

The ruler must know these five kinds of espionage.

This knowledge depends on the double spies.

Therefore, you must treat them with the utmost generosity.[13]

In ancient times, the rise of the Yin dynasty was due to I Chih, who served the house of Hsia;

the rise of the Chou dynasty was due to Lu Ya, who served the house of Yin.[14]

Therefore, enlightened rulers and good generals who are able to obtain intelligent agents as spies are certain for great achievements.

This is essential for warfare, and what the army depends on to move.[15]

Acknowledgments

As able as Sun Tzu was, even he needed allies, supporters, and friends. For *The Art of War—Spirituality for Conflict*, I had all three.

I believe that the very best people in the world are backing this book, and those behind the scenes at Skylight Paths Publishing, Sonshi.com, and Salesforce.com are to be commended first and foremost. Thank you all very much.

In addition, there are a few people I would like to individually recognize for their contribution to this book project:

Mark Ogilbee, my awesome editor at Skylight Paths. Intelligent, creative, and supportive, he is a credit to his profession. I was lucky to have worked with him side by side on this challenging book, and hope to work with him again very soon.

Dr. Thomas Cleary, author of over seventy-five books, and whom I consider not only a peerless scholar but also a wonderful teacher and friend. Who would have guessed the great Thomas Cleary, who inspired me to begin my study in The Art of War, would become a part of my own The Art of War twenty years later?

Marc Benioff, chairman and CEO of Salesforce.com, Inc. (NYSE: CRM), who has always been supportive of me and Sonshi.com. A consummate businessman, he is truly Sun Tzu's The Art of War in action and thus embodies the wisdom, honor, and compassion I expounded in this book. I am forever grateful for his kindness and friendship.

Carlye Adler, an award-winning journalist who collaborated with Marc Benioff and me on the Foreword. Friendly and knowledgeable—a true professional—she was a joy to work with.

Rabbi Rami Shapiro and Prof. Ron Miller, who, with extensive knowledge, reviewed my annotations containing Christian principles and amplified them with superb examples from the Hebrew Bible. I'm confident they will help me open and connect The Art of War to more readers who will inevitably discover that a Chinese work on warfare can indeed be applicable to their lives centered on love and peace.

Dr. Jay Abercrombie, world-renowned entomologist, ecologist, hiker, and author, and who I turn to regularly for advice. A constant voice of reason and wisdom, he also happens to be my father-in-law.

The following four individuals have literally defined my life. My wife, Samantha Huynh, a born leader who believed in me from the beginning. She is my best friend. My mother, Anne Marie Nguyen, whose courage and determination exemplify the Vietnamese ethos. Straight As on my report card rarely pleased her, but a simple phone call from me always did. My mentor, Willis Potts, a retired business executive and regent of the University System of Georgia. From his example, I learned firsthand how to effectively lead others by way of trust, empathy, and benevolence. My elementary school teacher Christine Franzke, who ignited my love of learning at an early age. It was an honor she reviewed my manuscript before publication.

Vu Huynh, my very cool tech-wizard brother, who was instrumental in the creation of the Sonshi.com website and making it the force it is now.

Special thanks go to John Ingram, chairman of Ingram Book Group, for giving me advice and encouragement just before I started writing this book, and who was also kind enough to have one of his top managers call me to explain the ins and outs of the book business.

A warm thank-you to Ted Grodhaus, Tom Madison, Rich Lieb, Kathy Anderson, and Becky Griffith at Skyline Steel–Arcelor Mittal for their support. Also, I owe dinners to Morris Rosenthal, Patrick Huynh, Nga Huynh, William Duiker, Pat Snook, Debbi Snook, and Pam Snook—all of them assisted me when I had questions.

And finally, my daughter, Victoria Huynh, and nephew, Dustin Truong, who serve as reminders to me of why I decided to write *The Art of War—Spirituality for Conflict* in the first place. Peace throughout the world is imminent with smart and caring children like them.

Notes

Front Cover

The military general faces a large contingent of red, angry enemies on the Chinese chess board. The leader who stands up against a sea of hatred will emerge victorious because of the formless, imperceptible, yet overwhelming force and strength *behind* him.

Introduction

1. Under the Wade-Giles romanization system first established in the 1860s, *The Art of War* is transliterated as "Ping Fa." *Ping Fa* literally means "Warfare Principles." The newer Pinyin system, approved by the Chinese government in 1958, transliterates the words as "Bing Fa."

2. A close Chinese pronunciation of *Sun Tzu* is SOON-zuh. The transliteration "Sun Tzu" is most commonly used and is from the Wade-Giles romanization system. In Pinyin the name is given as "Sun Zi."

3. Thomas Cleary, *The Art of War* (Boston: Shambhala Publications, 1988), 67, 128, 166.

4. As described by the Denma Translation Group's website www.victoryoverwar.com. Bestselling The Art of War author and scholar Ralph Sawyer wrote in his latest edition *The Essential Art of War* (Cambridge: Basic Books/Perseus Books Group, 2005), on page 131: "Although Web sites dedicated to Sun-tzu's thought and contemporary applicability continue to multiply, few have proved illuminating apart from Sonshi." In May 2007, a Sonshi.com reader even named his newborn daughter *Sonshi* (middle name) to commit himself to teaching her Sun Tzu's principles; this is perhaps our website's greatest honor and endorsement.

5. John Minford, *The Art of War: The Essential Translation of the Classic Book of Life* (New York: Viking/Penguin Group, 2002), liv.

6. J. H. Huang, *Sun Tzu: The New Translation* (New York: Quill, 1993), 20.

7. Steven Shankman and Stephen Durrant, *The Siren and the Sage: Knowledge and Wisdom in Ancient Greece and China* (London: Continuum International Publishing Group, 2000), 81.

8. Samuel B. Griffith, *The Art of War* (London: Oxford University Press, 1963), 57.
9. Sonshi.com's interview on February 26, 2004, and confirmed on telephone December 5, 2007, with William J. Duiker, biographer of Ho Chi Minh and author of *Ho Chi Minh: A Life* (New York: Hyperion Press, 2000). The interview can be accessed online at www.sonshi.com/duiker.html.
10. Henry David Thoreau, *The Thoughts of Thoreau,* ed. Edwin Way Teale (New York: Dodd, Mead & Company, 1987), 155. From Thoreau's *Journal*, written February 9, 1851.

Chapter 1—Calculations

14. "Those who are good": Derek Lin, *Tao Te Ching—Annotated & Explained* (Woodstock, VT: Skylight Paths Publishing, 2006), 137.
16. "Buddha believed": Ulrich Luz, Axel Michaels, and Linda Maloney, trans., *Encountering Jesus and Buddha: Their Lives and Teachings* (Minneapolis: Fortress Press, 2006), 86.

Chapter 2—Doing Battle

1. "horses were used only": Ralph D. Sawyer, *The Art of War* (Boulder: Westview Press, 1994), 37.
12. "Because you do not": Lin, *Tao Te Ching,* 45.

Chapter 3—Planning Attacks

1. "So when evenly matched": Ibid., 139.
7. "All-Under-Heaven": A Chinese cultural concept that denotes everyone and everything in the entire world, including enemies. The Chinese characters read *t'ien hsia*, which literally means "expanse above, people below."

Chapter 4—Formation

7. "Cyrus inquired": Nassim Nicholas Taleb, *Fooled by Randomness: The Hidden Role of Chance in Life and in the Markets* (New York: Random House, 2004), 3–4.

Chapter 5—Force

5. "the number five symbolizes": N. B. Dennys, *Folklore of China and Its Affinities with That of the Aryan and Semitic Races* (Whitefish, MT: Kessinger Publishing, 2003), 40.
9. "In using the military": Lin, *Tao Te Ching,* 139.

Chapter 6—Weakness and Strength

13. "the name *Viet Nam*": Sucheng Chan, *The Vietnamese American 1.5 Generation* (Philadelphia: Temple University Press, 2006) 4.
18. "Kenshin set the example": Stephen R. Turnbull, *The Samurai: A Military History* (London: RoutledgeCurzon, 2002), 120.

Chapter 7—Armed Struggle

12. "Book of Military Administration": Expressed by two eleventh-century scholars, Wang Hsi and Mei Yaochen, from the Sung dynasty. They were noted for their expertise in books of antiquity yet were unable to provide details on the apparently long-lost Book of Military Administration.
15. "You just keep loving people": Martin Luther King Jr., *The Papers of Martin Luther King, Jr.: Symbol of the Movement, January 1957–December 1958* (Berkeley: University of California Press, 2005), 4:321–322.

Chapter 8—Nine Changes

◆ "the number nine": Anne Birrell, *Chinese Mythology: An Introduction* (Baltimore: Johns Hopkins University Press, 1999), 71.
13. "Circumstances are not rigid": Thoreau, *The Thoughts of Thoreau*, 152. From Thoreau's letter to Harrison Blake (a former Unitarian minister and graduate of Harvard Divinity School), written March 27, 1848.

Chapter 9—Army Maneuvers

5. "a soldier carried his shield": Griffith, *The Art of War*, 117.
6. "According to Chinese legend": Yves Bonnefoy, *Asian Mythologies* (Chicago: University of Chicago Press, 1993), 246.
24. "It does not matter": Taleb, *Fooled by Randomness*, 4.

Chapter 10—Ground Formation

19. "The military is a tool": Lin, *Tao Te Ching*, 63.

Chapter 11—Nine Grounds

10. "If by setting one's heart": Yamamoto Tsunetomo, *Hagakure: The Book of the Samurai*, trans. William Scott Wilson (Tokyo: Kodansha International, 1979), 18.
30. "Huan Kung balked": Roger Ames, *The Art of War* (New York: Ballantine Books, 1993), 294.

33. "The Buddhist concept of *samadhi*": Akira Hirakawa, *A History of Indian Buddhism: From Sakyamuni to Early Mahayana,* trans. Paul Groner (New Delhi: Motilal Banarsidass Publishers, 1998), 301.

Chapter 12—Fire Attacks

3. "when the moon aligns": Huang, *Sun Tzu,* 108.

Chapter 13—Using Spies

14. "I Chih helped overthrow": Minford, *The Art of War,* 324.

Suggestions for Further Reading

Ames, Roger T. *The Art of War*. New York: Ballantine Books, 1993.

Benioff, Marc, and Carlye Adler. *The Business of Changing the World: Twenty Great Leaders on Strategic Corporate Philanthropy*. New York: McGraw-Hill, 2006.

Benioff, Marc, and Karen Southwick. *Compassionate Capitalism: How Corporations Can Make Doing Good an Integral Part of Doing Well*. Franklin Lakes, NJ: Career Press, 2004.

Cleary, Thomas. *The Art of War: Complete Texts and Commentaries*. Boston: Shambhala Publications, 2003.

———. *Mastering the Art of War: Zhuge Liang's and Liu Ji's Commentaries on the Classic by Sun Tzu*. Boston: Shambhala Publications, 1989.

———. *Zen Lessons: The Art of Leadership*. Boston: Shambhala Publications, 1989.

Denma Translation Group. *The Art of War: A New Translation*. Boston: Shambhala Publications, 2001.

Griffith, Samuel B. *The Art of War*. London: Oxford University Press, 1963.

Huang, J. H. *Sun Tzu: The New Translation*. New York: Quill, 1993.

Lin, Derek. *Tao Te Ching—Annotated & Explained*. Woodstock, VT: Skylight Paths Publishing, 2006.

Minford, John. *The Art of War: The Essential Translation of the Classic Book of Life*. New York: Viking, 2002.

Sawyer, Ralph D. *The Seven Military Classics of Ancient China*. Boulder: Westview Press, 1993.

———. *The Tao of War: The Martial Tao Te Ching*. Boulder: Westview Press, 2003.

Taleb, Nassim Nicholas. *Fooled by Randomness: The Hidden Role of Chance in Life and in the Markets*. New York: Random House, 2004.

In addition, I personally invite you to www.sonshi.com, an educational website for those interested in learning more about Sun Tzu's The Art of War. Endorsed by over forty major The Art of War authors and scholars, its purpose is to help you apply the book's concepts and principles correctly. Dallas Galvin, editor of the Barnes & Noble Classics edition *The Art of War* (Barnes & Noble Books, 2003) wrote on page 271 of his book that Sonshi.com is "The best site for newly minted aficionados. With book reviews, news bulletins, and a conversational tone, it is the most accessible." Our online community has over one thousand topics related to The Art of War, over five thousand reader-generated commentaries for all verses, and serves over one million unique visitors around the world annually—all without spam or advertisements.

About SKYLIGHT PATHS Publishing

SkyLight Paths Publishing is creating a place where people of different spiritual traditions come together for challenge and inspiration, a place where we can help each other understand the mystery that lies at the heart of our existence.

Through spirituality, our religious beliefs are increasingly becoming a part of our lives—rather than *apart* from our lives. While many of us may be more interested than ever in spiritual growth, we may be less firmly planted in traditional religion. Yet, we do want to deepen our relationship to the sacred, to learn from our own as well as from other faith traditions, and to practice in new ways.

SkyLight Paths sees both believers and seekers as a community that increasingly transcends traditional boundaries of religion and denomination—people wanting to learn from each other, *walking together, finding the way.*

For your information and convenience, at the back of this book we have provided a list of other SkyLight Paths books you might find interesting and useful. They cover the following subjects:

www.ingramcontent.com/pod-product-compliance
Lightning Source LLC
Chambersburg PA
CBHW030728150426
42813CB00051B/326